*Widows
Among
Us*

Widows Among Us

Stories and Insights

KAREN S. JUSTICE, MBA

KAREN R. SMITH-RACICOT, CLC

REBECCA K. LaCHANCE, PhD

Dedications

Rebecca LaChance
To Frank, for your presence, your love, and your laugh, which always made me smile.
To my mom, for providing the foundation for who I became.

Karen Justice
To John, for all the shared love, challenges, and adventures that prepared and enabled me to live the life I now have.

Karen Smith Racicot
To Sam, for the wisdom you imparted while with us and the lessons you helped us learn after your death.

From us all
To all the widows we know and the widows we will know.

As a woman strolled along the familiar path,
she encountered an unexpected fork in the road.
One path of the fork vanished into thin air,
lost in the space between heartbeats,
while the other stretched out before her.

This new fork seems to swirl in grief and sorrow.
How will she navigate this path to a place of joy,
light, laughter, and the hope of better days?

As she looks to her side,
she sees the glow of thousands of women
—the widows among us—
surrounding her and sharing what she needs to move forward.
They guide her, for these women have been to this place
and know there is a way through,
a way to overcome.

—Rebecca K. LaChance

Table of Contents

Preface

Sobering Statistics

According to Kiplinger Personal Finance, more than one million women join America's nearly fifteen million widows and widowers each year. (2021)

+ According to the U.S. Census Bureau, the median age for a woman to become a widow is 59.4 for a first marriage and 60.3 for a second marriage. (May 2021)

+ One-third of widows became widows before age sixty, while half of married women will become widows by age sixty-five. (WISER: Women's Institute for a Secure Retirement)

+ Half of widows over sixty-five will outlive their husbands by fifteen years.

+ According to the United Nations, in June 2022, there were an estimated 258 million widows worldwide.

This Book Is for You

You may not realize it, but chances are you will be a widow someday. Whatever the reason for your widowhood, this book is for you.

Are you a younger woman with visions of forty or fifty years of a future with your partner? Life is unpredictable, and you might not have as much time together as you'd like. We have written this book to provide hope and support for those going through the experience of becoming a widow. Our goal is to convey the message that despite the challenges, your future can be filled with brightness and optimism.

This book has multiple parts. In Part One, we tell our personal stories of widowhood. We are three women with unique experiences and reactions to becoming widows and eventually transforming into stronger, engaging selves. We share the most challenging parts: our responses, actions, and choices. We show the power of intentional friendships. We explore the growth we've had throughout the process. We conclude Part One with a brief summary of what we learned and how those insights aided us.

Part Two outlines the preparations necessary in the early days of your marriage or as soon as possible. This book is not a definitive treatise on widowhood. It describes not only our own experiences but also the lived experiences of widows who responded to our survey and interviews. We interviewed dozens of widows until the responses reached saturation. It is not meant to be an academic study.

Other widows also shared numerous anecdotes, providing a shared pool of information. This confirmed the universality of widowhood and each woman's unique experience.

From this collective information, you will find suggestions, ideas, reassurances, and confirmations. They do not constitute professional advice in any way. Please consult a professional advisor for details on any of these suggestions and how they affect your specific circumstance.

As you'll see, our results indicated that many women needed to prepare early in their married lives to take on every detail of their homes, businesses, finances, and friendships.

One of our most significant findings was that women were financially, legally, or logistically unprepared. This section offers practical information to minimize stress and ease the transition into the widow's new future.

We wholeheartedly recommend that every woman acts in her best interests BEFORE being thrown into the tornado of death and its impacts. The most relevant thing we can do is to teach our daughters to be widows before it happens so that younger generations are not as unprepared as many widows have been.

Part Three speaks directly to the widowed individual. It covers experiences such as dealing with brain fog and taking care of oneself while managing the demands, stresses, and health issues that come with being a widow. It also discusses ways to understand and cope with different emotions, make choices about friendship, find new love, and explain why a widow might accidentally call her new love by her late husband's name.

Part Four provides information for the new widow's family and friends. They may find it challenging to know what to say or do or when to help. This section provides guidance and support for them.

If you have recently been widowed, it's understandable that you may not feel ready to read anything at the moment. We totally understand because we have been in the same situation. We suggest keeping the book close to your bedside. Even if you read just a paragraph per day, we strongly believe our stories will help you in some way. We invite you to read any section as needed. Feel free to skip around the contents to find the information you need or want. Eventually, there will come a time when you will be able to read for longer periods.

Our experiences as widows occurred when our children were already grown. It's important to acknowledge that we may not be able to provide insight into the challenges of caring for young children and teens after a parent's passing. Additionally, we understand that the profound and life-altering effects of violence-related deaths are experiences beyond our own. While we aim to offer helpful information to widows, we recognize that our personal experiences cannot fully encompass these particular circumstances.

Widower? Though we have written from our voices as widows, much of the information is also helpful to men.

Our goal is to convey that there is no single way to grieve or heal from one of life's most traumatic events. Our intention is to help you recognize that your grieving process is valid and that you will eventually be all right. You don't have to conform to anyone else's predetermined path or expectations about grieving, surviving, and thriving.

◘   ◘   ◘

Meet Rebecca
and the Two Karens

As if we were an amateur rock band, we have been called "Rebecca and the Two Karens." While it's true that we've been on a few tours together, the keyboards we use don't make music; they create words. However, like band members, we share similar experiences and outlooks, yet we are very different women. Age and appearance are the apparent differences. Karen Smith-Racicot is six feet tall and blond. Karen Justice barely manages to reach five feet and is a redhead. Rebecca LaChance is five-foot-eight with a crown of white hair. Tall Karen was sixty, Rebecca was seventy-one, and Short Karen was seventy-five as we began writing this book. Our other commonality is that we are widows.

The two Karens were both members of a local women's business organization. Rebecca traveled in the same business circles as the Karens but kept to herself. Short Karen and Rebecca had met through a mutual friend. When Short Karen posted an announcement on Facebook in 2019 that she was organizing a group tour to Morocco, Rebecca, Tall Karen, and her second husband, Bob, were part of the small group who signed up. At the time of the trip, the Karens were widows. Tall Karen had been widowed in 2010. Short Karen was widowed in 2017. Rebecca was still married to the man who had been a gift in her life.

On day ten of the tour, a Moroccan spa in Essaouira, Morocco, was on the itinerary. The three of us found ourselves in a small tiled room being soaped, scrubbed, and then placed in the middle of the room to be hosed off. We didn't know each other very well before the trip, yet here we were: totally nude and accidentally more intimate than we had ever anticipated. Rebecca commented that we were the only ones to see her tattoo except for her husband.

That day, we bonded. Little did we know how that bond would change and grow from naked derrières to supporting Rebecca as she entered the process of widowhood a year later.

During a wildly energetic winter trip to Sedona a few years later, we wrapped ourselves in blankets as we savored a glass of wine by the porch fireplace, with the red rocks rising before us. The idea of writing a book for other widows sprouted in our consciousness as we shared our experiences and wisdom with each other. Since that time, we have exposed our fears, our vulnerabilities, and our souls to each other. We hope that by sharing many of those with you, we provide some form of guidance and reassurance for your widowhood.

Yet, it's been an emotionally difficult road for all three of us to get to where we are.

Our stories hold the truths of our complex lives and are shared with the fullness of our pain and our movement into the light of wisdom and joyful adventures.

There were undoubtedly days we might not have believed in the possibility of wisdom and joyful adventures. Yet, that wisdom has built in us the understanding of how universal this life experience is. Just as our stories are part of all other stories of widowhood, your story will connect you to us.

Welcome!

PART ONE

Three Windows into Widowhood

Stories from the Three Widowed Authors

Sam and Karen, Vermont, Celebrating their 25th wedding anniversary, November 2009.

Tall Karen's Story

"In this world, nothing can be said to be certain except death and taxes."
—Ben Franklin

Monday, Monday

The tax deadline was looming as I entered the office that Monday morning, April 12, 2010. My husband Sam and I had owned the tax and accounting business for twenty years, but with more than five hundred clients, the stress of tax season never got easier. We were both looking forward to the April 15 deadline so we would have a chance to relax, regroup, and focus on other aspects of our lives. Our three daughters—Shannon, Danielle, and Jessica—were at a crossroads in their college lives, and we wanted to be able to concentrate on helping them. But first—three more days until relief.

Sam and I had spent an unusually relaxing weekend together—rare during this time of the year. So that morning, I was in a good mood when I kissed him goodbye and left the house. He had worked late into the night and was sleeping in.

A few hours later, my office manager, Cindi, asked me when to expect him. She had questions about a tax return he had left for her to assemble. I was surprised he wasn't in yet, knowing how busy we would be. The office was bustling with last-minute phone calls and client visits. The morning passed quickly, but there was still no Sam.

When two police officers entered the office at 12:50, I knew something terrible had happened. My heart shattered into a million pieces as they told me that Sam had had a massive heart attack while driving to work, and died instantly. My husband, best friend, and business partner was dead at the age of forty-nine. I was a widow at forty-seven. My entire world turned upside down.

My staff gathered around me when I came out of the conference room. "Sam," I said, choking up, "had a massive heart attack on the way to work this morning. He's . . . dead." I could barely get the words out past the lump in my throat. The shock was evident from everyone—Sam was loved and respected by the employees, and his sudden loss cut us all to the core.

I was in a daze, but I knew instinctively that everyone would look to me for guidance in Sam's absence in the upcoming days and weeks. I took some deep, gulping breaths. "We have a tax deadline in three days," I said calmly. "The clients will understand; the IRS will not. Our number one priority is ensuring that all tax returns are filed or extended." I had complete faith that my staff would do what needed to be done and that my admin staff of Cindi and Mary Ann would be sure to tie up any loose ends.

Cindi began looking into flight options to get Shannon and Danielle home from their respective colleges. Jessica was living at home and attending the community college, so she would be the first of the girls to know.

Mary Ann called my mother to ask her to come into the office, but she hung up a few times before she could gather herself enough to speak. We were all in such a state of shock.

My mother came immediately to the office. As she walked in, I blurted out, "Mom—Sam's dead." I sobbed. She wrapped me in a hug as I told her what the officers had told me.

I called Sam's brother. "Todd, something terrible has happened. Sam—" I took a deep breath. "Sam had a massive heart attack on his way to work today. He's—dead." I swallowed a big lump of tears. "Please break the news to your mom. I'm heading home shortly." Todd didn't say much then, but I knew the news was devastating, as he had always looked up to his big brother.

My heart was heavy as I drove home. My dad had died unexpectedly six months prior, and I kept thinking about how I had lost the two most important men in my life in just six months. I was close to my two brothers, but they lived out of state and weren't here for the day-to-day part of our lives. My mom, daughters, and I were the only ones left in the area.

Since my dad's death, I had been helping my mom navigate her new life as a widow, including how to adjust her budget after losing two-thirds of her income. Now, I was faced with the reality of many of the same hurdles she was dealing with. And I kept remembering a conversation with my mom shortly after my dad died:

"I don't know what I would do if anything ever happened to Sam," I had said to my mom. "I couldn't survive."

"You'd figure it out," she said to me. "It's hard, but you could do it."

"No, I couldn't," I insisted. "He's my entire world. I couldn't survive without him. I wouldn't know what to do." I truly believed that, and now, I was terrified of facing a future without him.

Jessica was home when I arrived. I started sobbing as soon as I saw her, and she knew something terrible had happened. When I told her, her first concern was her sisters.

"Have you told Shannon and Danielle yet?" she asked.

"No, I'm preparing to do that now," I answered. "I just don't know how I'm going to tell them," I said sadly.

It was two of the hardest phone calls I'd have to make in my life. As a mom, I wanted to protect my daughters from pain, but that was impossible. I had arranged for someone at Danielle's dorm to be with her when I told her. Because of Shannon's reaction after my dad died, I knew she would want to hear the news when she was alone.

"Shannon," I said, with a catch in my voice. "Your dad . . . " There was a long pause. "He had a heart attack."

"Okay," she said slowly. A pause.

"Shannon, he had a heart attack," I repeated, fighting back the tears.

"Okay," she said again. I could hear her pacing back and forth in her room, the tension palpable with the unasked question—what's his condition?

"Shannon, he's dead."

"NO!" She screamed and burst into tears. I heard her run down the stairs and out the door toward the small lake near her house. I knew she could walk around there, and no one would hear her hysterical crying—no one except me, who was still on the other end of the line.

"Shannon. Shannon!" I said, trying to keep myself together. "Please! I need you to calm down. Listen, this is really important. Please calm down."

She took a deep breath. "Okay," she said, with a sharp intake of breath. "I am calm."

I gave her the information for the flight that would bring her home that evening. She would make the necessary arrangements to get to the airport.

All three girls were in shock. At eighteen and twenty-one years of age, they were old enough to have learned a lot from their dad but young enough to still have so much more to learn. It ripped my heart out when I thought about how the girls and I would no longer have his humor and wisdom in our lives. We would never again be annoyed at his exuberance of waking us up in the morning, or roll our eyes at the ridiculous practical jokes he would play. All we had left now were memories.

My office manager, Cindi, was a rock to me during that time. She made sure that the office continued to function correctly: handling hundreds of tax extensions, explanations to many of our over five hundred clients, and everything else I did not have the emotional fortitude to handle.

Friends began to stop by as the word spread. Everyone expressed their shock and disbelief, often at a loss for words.

My brother, Ken, flew in from Oregon. My brother, Jeff, and sister-in-law, Fran, came from Georgia. My mom was with me constantly, and my mother-in-law, Nancy, gave me the support she could through her own grief. She had lost her husband when she was forty-six, so she knew what I was going through.

The Early Years

Sam had been a dairy farmer in Frederick County, Maryland, when we were introduced by mutual friends in 1982. I was a junior at Shepherd University. Sam had attended the University of Maryland on a full scholarship, but his dad died in the middle of his second year, so he came home to run the farm. We married after I graduated from college in 1984, and I got a job forty-five minutes away.

I switched to part-time work after our first daughter, Shannon, was born in March 1988. A month later, Sam took a giant leap of faith and sold the dairy cows. It was out of character for me to take risks, but I took his hand, closed my eyes, and made the leap of faith with him.

Money was tight. My mom found an ad for a tax preparer in the home office of an accounting franchise. Sam, who had experience preparing farm taxes, was a perfect match for the franchise owners with farming clients.

After the first tax season, Sam joined the local Frederick franchisee. He had loved the business and financial aspect of running his farm and was excited to work with other business owners. Since the franchise also needed help with office work, I quit my job down the road and began working part-time for the franchise. Both decisions were another leap of faith, as we were now dependent on the income Sam generated in an unfamiliar office environment.

In the meantime, Sam and I talked about having more children. I had always wanted three or four, but Sam knew he would need to work long and hard to build his part of the business to create a life for us, so he only wanted to have one more. His comment to me was, "If you want three kids, you better hope the next one's twins!" A year later, we had twin girls! Jessica and Danielle came into our lives in June 1991.

In the spring of 1992, I grasped Sam's hand tightly and took yet another leap of faith as we decided to branch out with our own franchise.

Over the next eighteen years, the business had many ups and downs, but with Sam's guidance, it continued to grow and provide our family with a beautiful life. We began in the basement of our home with just one employee—my dad, who had retired early from the government—and eventually expanded to our final location in Middletown, Maryland, with a team of twelve to fifteen employees. As the office manager, I was blessed over those years to work my own schedule, allowing me to be home with the girls after school and involved in their activities.

Back to the Misery

It was day two of misery. My mom, mother-in-law Nancy, my daughters, and I were at the church, discussing funeral details with Pastor Kathy. Danielle volunteered to play her flute, accompanied by her friend Krista on the piano. Sam and I had loved hearing Danielle play, so it would add a lovely element to the service. Shannon had a quote and story she wanted to read, and Jessica would accompany and support her.

After meeting with Pastor Kathy, the girls and I met with the funeral director to decide on the viewing and other arrangements. We chose the coffin, the final resting place of my beloved Sam. It was almost more than I could take. But it had to be done.

My emotions were all over the place as I looked through photos to create a slideshow to play during the viewing—pictures of Sam that showed our life together, a shared life that had ended early and abruptly.

The future was a vast, looming black cloud. Supportive people surrounded me, and their presence helped keep my anxiety about the future at bay. But the anxiety was like a constant dull headache—always there, but less intrusive if I was busy. However, it was back in full force any time I stopped and had a moment of silence.

Saying Goodbye

Sam was very involved in the community and a well-known accountant, so we knew there would be a large crowd at the viewing. Ironically, the day was April 15. It should have been our busiest workday of the year when the whole office bustled furiously to meet the tax deadline. But this year, the employees finished their work early and came to acknowledge their former boss, sharing their respect for this great man.

Shannon and Jessica stayed close by my side near the coffin that night and helped me greet people as they came through the line. The girls were my rock, helping to keep me steady. Danielle was my social butterfly, greeting the seemingly endless stream of people as they came in.

"Karen, how are we going to make it without him?" asked one of our longtime clients, who was close to Sam. We hugged each other and cried for the huge, gaping hole that Sam's death would make in both of our lives, each of us wondering how to proceed without his guidance.

A good high school friend drove the five-hour round trip to be there for me. "Ellen!" I exclaimed, seeing her. "I can't believe you came all this way!" I couldn't stop crying and hugged her so tightly, not wanting to let go. She is one of the strongest women I know. She has been through a lot in her life, losing her dad a few weeks before her marriage at twenty-two and her mom six months before the birth of her first child. She is divorced, and she has no family support around her, so she has had to create a life for herself and her two children on an assistant teacher's salary. I have always admired her spirit and fortitude despite life's setbacks. I knew that I'd need to rely on her strength in the future to help me move forward.

People came to shake our hands, to convey their condolences and sorrow, and to wish us strength. I was grateful for their presence and sentiments, yet it was hard to get through the fog swirling in my brain. They came to look one last time at the man who had somehow touched their lives and said the same thing in so many different ways. And it was sincere and heartfelt. It was meant to be comforting, but there was no comfort to be found. There was only the constant repetition that you have lost someone dear. At the end of the day, all I knew was that far too many people loved Sam to make his early departure at all fair or just. I could not think of anything more. If I did, my soul might have shattered from the pain.

The next day was the funeral. The setting was hauntingly familiar—hadn't we just done this exact thing just a short six months ago for my father? Many of the same people were there, just as stunned as we were. Why were we here again so soon, going through the process of saying goodbye to another good man who was such an integral part of our lives?

Sam's brother Todd went up to say a few words. It was short and heartfelt and magnificent for this moment. "I . . . I've been sober a few years now," he declared to the church. "I've actually done it this time. I don't know if Sam knew that . . . I hope he did. You know, he was always there for me. He was my inspiration to be better, and I really hope he knew that I was doing better. I kept my promise this time."

Todd breathed in and continued, "My brother was a great man, and I never really told him that enough. But he is the only reason that I am still here today." He bowed his head in sadness and returned to sit beside his mother.

Shannon and Jessica stood proudly at the front of the church, sharing Shannon's story about her dad. When it was Danielle's turn, her friend Krista sat at the piano, and Danielle faced the church to play her flute. They played "You Raise Me Up." Danielle's flute was hauntingly beautiful, but near the end, she broke down and started to cry, unable to get a sound out of the flute. Krista continued to play the piano until Danielle could compose herself and finish the song. There wasn't a dry eye in the entire church when they finished.

Pastor Kathy stood up at the podium. "It is said, 'There will always be death and taxes, but we find that taxes come too often and death comes too soon.'" She let that line reverberate heavily around the church. She then recited the lyrics from the Mamas and the Papas song, "Monday, Monday."

I began sobbing. That song would forever be imprinted on my brain and invoke sorrow anytime I heard it. Why did these words exist to remind me of how instantly life can change?

At the reception following the service, I walked around and visited with everyone. I appreciated them coming and knew that their love and support would get me through the next few days and weeks. I wouldn't let myself think beyond that.

I ran into Sam's high school friends, including his best friend Randy. We recently got together after a long hiatus. I suggested that we should make an effort to meet up more frequently because life is short, and we never know what tomorrow may bring. Little did we know that sentiment would become relevant again all too soon.

More Losses

A few weeks after Sam's funeral, my friend Laurie called me.

"Karen?" Laurie said. "Are you sitting down? I have some terrible news. I'm so sorry to tell you, but Randy died over the weekend from a heart attack. I'm so sorry!"

"This can't be real. This can't be happening. Not Randy, too!" I exclaimed. I started to cry. I railed against God, against fate, against everything. First, my father. Just a short six months later, my beloved Sam. And now Randy? I sat in the chair in my bedroom, arms wrapped around my knees, rocking and crying. I eventually called my brother Jeff because I couldn't stand being alone for one more second. I could do little more than cry, but having him on the other end of the phone was enough.

Still, there were more losses to come. Another friend in our group of six couples died nine months later of cancer. Three men under the age of fifty, leaving widows of the same age. Eighteen months later, another friend's husband died suddenly of a heart attack. He was sixty-two. The losses were beyond heartbreaking.

Personalities

Sam looked at every challenge as an opportunity to make something better. He once told me that he loved knowing that he could make a difference in someone's life every day. But I never understood how knowing the tax laws would make a difference in *anyone's* life. It was long after his death before I understood that it wasn't about the tax laws. It was about listening to and believing in people, and encouraging them to pursue their dreams. What Sam knew instinctively would take me time to understand.

I, on the other hand, focused on problems and stressed enough for both of us. I had always struggled with self-confidence and would do almost *anything* not to be noticed. I created the workflow processes in the office and trained my admin staff to make sure they were implemented. I had a sixth sense of how to make the business run better. But because all of this came so easily to me, I didn't see it as a significant contribution. As our accounting business grew, I shifted more and more of my responsibility to others. The less I did, the more my confidence decreased, along with my sense of self-worth. I began to see myself as unimportant and retreated into a comfort zone.

Unlike Sam, I did not find it easy to converse with others. Whenever I went anywhere with him, I let him carry the conversation while I hung back. When I walked into a room, I looked for the safest place to go to observe and eventually picked a "safe" person to talk to, never letting my guard down.

Between my lack of confidence and the attention that Sam commanded just by being himself, I became lost. I felt as though, other than my girls, my mom, and the "running" of the business (which I knew someone else could do as well), I wasn't important and had no purpose in life.

Sam constantly encouraged me to try new things—classes at the local college or interacting with friends—but the fear of not being good enough held me back. The less I interacted with others, the less confidence I had. It was a vicious cycle from which I could not break free. And yet, no one knew the depths of my loneliness and despair. Looking back, I realize the edge of depression was my constant companion. On the outside, I seemed like a happy, confident person. But inside, I was nothing.

Major Decisions

With Sam's death, I was totally unprepared for decisions about the house and the business and what I was going to do with my life in the future, alone.

I knew we were woefully unprepared for an unexpected life event. There was minimal life insurance, and we had never had a "what if" conversation. I did not want to think of a life without Sam, so I refused even to have a conversation with him. My thinking was that I'd sell the business, sell the house, and buy a small condo where I could lock myself away from the world because it would be too hard without him. Now that reality had happened, I longed for those conversations so I could still have his guidance and wisdom to help me. But I was on my own.

I was determined that Sam's death wouldn't derail the girls' plans. It was important to me that Jessica and Danielle continued with college and that Shannon made whatever decision she needed to after graduation. The grit and determination of all three were humbling to me. They all got stellar grades during this time and never once used this tragedy as an excuse not to do well. The love and pride I felt for them, even today, is beyond expression.

Our house had been a dream purchase—a log home in the mountains, away from the hustle and bustle of life. Sam and I loved to sit on the front porch or back deck, enjoying only the sounds of nature and the company of each other and our dogs. Without Sam, I couldn't imagine being alone in that large, distant house and the upkeep it required. We had bought the house at the height of the market in 2007, and now, in 2010, my options were very limited, as the value was well below the mortgage balance and the housing market was stagnant. I decided to put the house on the market, even though I knew it most likely wouldn't sell. However, making that decision gave me a sense of relief and hope.

The business was tricky. I knew it was essential to decide quickly whether to sell or continue it on my own. The clients had their own businesses to think about and couldn't wait too long for my decision. But I couldn't see how it was even remotely possible for me to continue the business alone without Sam. Sam generated over 70 percent of the income, so the bottom line was sure to take a hit immediately. The pressure of the decision was a crushing weight.

In some ways, I felt like I had been given the rare opportunity to choose the direction of my life—no spouse to consider, kids on their own, house up for sale. The only thing I had to decide about was the business; keep it and continue on the same path forward, or sell it and choose from unlimited options.

The idea of having the freedom to choose whatever I wanted seemed attractive at first. I could go anywhere, do anything, and be anyone I wanted. But the thought of that soon became more frightening than trying to run the business. At least with the business, I felt secure knowing what to do and how to do it. If I sold it, I would have to take full responsibility for myself, my decisions, and the consequences that came with them. I had no idea how I was going to manage everything on my own, especially a freedom that was unfamiliar to me.

After many emotional conversations and breaking down my "I can't do this!" arguments, my brother Ken and daughter Shannon finally convinced me to keep the business. They knew it was my lack of confidence in myself that didn't allow me to believe I could do it, but they also knew I had an excellent staff and twenty years of experience running it with Sam and that the clients knew and trusted me. I hired a CPA to take over most of Sam's duties and took the plunge, but I was still terrified.

The clients were thrilled that I was keeping the business. Although I kept up a good façade for everyone, I often felt like a fraud. Learning more about the tax and accounting laws and helping clients understand how these laws affected their business was a heavy responsibility for me. My lack of confidence didn't help.

"I can't do this. I just can't! It's so hard!" was a part of my typical conversation with Shannon after attending a tax seminar. "I don't understand half of what they are talking about, and I'll never remember it all!" I would cry to her. Everything was overwhelming—the tax laws, the rules and regulations, and the fear of doing something wrong and having the IRS come after me or, worse yet, a client. However, I kept pushing forward against what felt like a brick wall. The bricks were the overwhelming information I was learning, held together by the mortar of my insecurities.

Our First Milestone

Shannon's graduation from the College of Charleston was less than a month after Sam's death. She was allotted only four tickets to graduation and had fretted over this last fall, as it had been one short for our family. With my dad's death, an extra ticket became unnecessary. With Sam's death, she had an extra one.

The graduation ceremony was a lovely Charleston event, with graduates dressed in white dresses or tuxes, with red roses or boutonnieres. I fought back tears as I watched Shannon cross the stage, proudly wearing her honors stole and medallions representing her accomplishments. I know how proud Sam was of all three of our girls going to college, and my heart was breaking that he was not there to witness Shannon's—and ultimately Danielle's or Jessica's—graduations. It was the perfect day to celebrate her accomplishments and forget, just for a moment, the pain and grief that were our constant companions.

Life Keeps Plodding Along

I often wanted to scream to no one in particular, "Why don't you care that my life has been ripped to shreds? Why hasn't the world stopped to acknowledge that someone magnificent has just left it?" But life continued on, plodding its way through each day with no acknowledgment of my loss. The normalcy and routines of life are what got me through the day, but sometimes, I felt that it would have been better if life had somehow given me a sign that it was devastated, too. It didn't, so I continued on, smiling when I could and crying when it became too much.

My strongest motivation to get out of bed every morning and keep putting one foot in front of the other was my girls. I didn't want them to worry about me, and I knew that they would face challenges in their own life. I wanted to show them that no matter how difficult things got or what life threw their way, they could say, "Yes, life is tough right now. But look at what Mom was able to do after Dad's death. If she can do it, so can I." That motivation is what kept me going, day in and day out, pushing me forward when I wanted to crawl back into my comfort zone, a really small place where I didn't have to take responsibility for anything.

Releasing Anger

"Those fucking men!" I raged to myself as I took another swing with my hammer at the trampoline frame, tears almost blinding me. "Good-for-nothings!" I continued, in rhythm with the hammer. "Why do I even bother thinking that they'll be helpful? I should know by now that if I want something done, I need to do it myself!" *Bam! Bam! Bam!* My rage came through with each hammer swing, along with the frustration and the reality that I was going to have to take care of things myself instead of shifting them to others.

The trampoline had been a gift to the girls, and they had loved it. But they were now all in college, so I wanted it gone. I had asked Sam to take it down when the twins left for college in the fall of 2009. It wasn't a priority for him, so it didn't get done. After his death, I had asked my brothers to help me take it down when they were in town, but again, other things always grabbed their attention more. So, one day, I had had enough of the "incompetence of men" and decided to take matters into my own hands—literally. That's how I found myself in June, beating the living hell out of it.

"Scott," I said over the phone, my anger about men having been spent for the moment. "I've taken our trampoline apart. Since the men in my life couldn't get it done even after I'd asked them to, I took matters into my own hands. It is in pieces on the ground in our yard, where I beat it to death, getting it apart. I'd appreciate it if you could come by with your truck sometime to get rid of it."

"Okay . . . ," he said, without questioning my statement. He could tell that I was frustrated. Two days later, it was gone, and I was grateful.

The experience was a release of anger for me and another turning point. I had always made Sam take care of these types of things. They weren't a priority for him, so often he wouldn't get to it for a while, which was frustrating to me and added to my victim mentality. I had seen myself as unable to do them, but I would get angry at him for not following my agenda. Now, I knew that I could figure out how to get things done—and even use up energy doing it.

My Confidence Journey

Within a few months of Sam's death, I surprised myself by making bold accessory choices, like choosing a lime green nail color for a pedicure and a bright red purse to carry. Later, I got a purple streak in my hair. I had typically made conservative choices when it came to dressing and accessories—primarily so that I wouldn't stand out in the crowd any more than my six-one height made me. Although I felt a disconnect between my new choices on the outside and who I was on the inside, the bold outside choices showed confidence. Maybe, just maybe, that could translate into confidence on the inside.

I had not yet internalized that outside confidence. On my first trip alone after Sam's death, my insecurities were running rampant. "Why did I ever decide to do this? Why, oh, why didn't I look this up before I came? What am I going to do?" My anxiety was out of control and threatening to bubble over. I wanted to curl into a ball on the floor and cry, but since I was in the middle of the Boston airport, I needed to maintain control of my spiraling emotions.

I had to get to a hotel for a business conference I was attending, but I could not find the number for the hotel shuttle. I asked at the help desk, but the person had a foreign accent and I couldn't understand him clearly in my emotional state. The more times I asked, the more I could feel panic rising until I had to walk away before I turned into a blubbering idiot.

"I'm an intelligent person. I can figure this out," I kept repeating to myself as I stared blindly out the window of the terminal. I could hear people passing behind me, but I tuned them out. "Just breathe." And I did. In, out. In, out. Over and over again, I took deep breaths until I could feel myself calm down enough to think straight.

"Okay, what do I need to do?" I asked myself. "I know the hotel. How can I find out how to get there? Think about it—you can do this." In, out. In, out.

"Call the hotel!" It turned out there was no shuttle; I'd have to take a taxi. Okay, problem solved, and one tiny but significant boost in my confidence. I realized I wasn't stupid, just unprepared.

Now for the next hurdle—the convention itself. It was hosted by the software company our office used, and I knew it would be beneficial to attend. However, I also knew it would be a huge stretch for me to attend something where I didn't know anyone. I had to figure out not only the logistics of the convention but also how to interact with and talk to people without Sam taking the lead. Typically, it was my worst nightmare.

By the time I got to my hotel room, I was exhausted and wanted to be alone. But I had made arrangements to have a drink with my software salesman, so I went down to the bar after refreshing myself. It was a pleasant evening, and I was grateful I had made the connection before I got there, forcing me to follow through. Looking back, I realized that advance planning was a move that I was to make many times, unconsciously building my confidence every step of the way. I knew I wouldn't back out, and it would force me to interact with people. A small but significant step toward gaining confidence.

I was still feeling overwhelmed by the tax and accounting laws, so I found myself struggling to maintain the newfound confidence that was starting to blossom within me. When I was on my way to visit a tax client, an older couple I had never met, my usual fears and insecurities began to overshadow it and I couldn't stop the doubts swirling in my head.

In the end, I spent two delightful hours with this couple. I was grateful for their compassion and love for Sam and for their open acceptance of me. This experience gave me another boost in confidence.

When I reflected on some of the meetings I'd had since Sam died, I realized that the clients were encouraging me and respected what I had to say. I would have conversations with them about their business—regular, everyday conversations that Sam and I had about ours. It wasn't up to me to gain their trust; I already had it because Sam had laid the path, and I continued to keep it through my interactions with them. I was still not a fan of the tax laws, but that's why I had a staff—they took care of the tax and accounting work, and I needed to know enough to have intelligent conversations with the clients. I ultimately came to love the interactions with the clients.

Day by day, little by little, I was making progress. Who I was becoming—confident, more outgoing—was always there but buried beneath my fear and lack of confidence. I now understand what Sam meant when he said, "Karen, I believe in you. You can do it." Finally, I was starting to believe him.

Gaining Confidence Through Other Women

I had attended a few meetings of a local women's group, Wholistic Women Retreats, and I was invited to an overnight retreat they were having in the fall of 2010. The topics would include self-care, gaining confidence, and others that I truly needed to hear. I knew the women were inviting and nonjudgmental, so I kept telling myself I would be okay. In my heart, I knew that was true, but years of thinking I was inferior were hard to overcome. I said yes, but with reservations. Was I truly ready for this?

I got a single room because I knew I'd need an escape when I felt overwhelmed by the togetherness. Typically, when I was with people I didn't know well, I could feel the fear of conversing almost paralyzing me. I would stay silent, withdrawing into myself. This weekend, however, I found myself engaging in group conversations and interacting with women I didn't know.

The retreat was encouraging with the unconditional acceptance these ladies practiced. I never felt stupid or less than. As the weekend went on, there was a boost in my self-confidence, especially when I heard one woman say, "I guess this means I have to pick up that thousand-pound phone and call people." WOW! I wasn't the only one who had an aversion to the phone! I was constantly berating myself because it seemed so easy for everyone else. But even these women, whom I thought had it all together, struggled with this! The crack continued to widen in my wall of "not good enough" that I had always used to protect myself.

With another local women's group I really gained my confidence and grew into my leadership abilities. It all started with my friend Joyce, who was always looking out for me. She introduced me to Caroline, a business owner who had suddenly lost her husband a few years prior. She and I had lunch and talked about loss, owning a business while going through this trauma, and looking toward our next chapter in life. Caroline invited me to an event hosted by an organization she was involved in—Women's Business Network (WBN) of Frederick, Maryland.

It was difficult to say yes because these situations still caused me anxiety. Although I was meeting Caroline there, I couldn't expect her to be by my side the entire evening. I'd have to interact with these unknown women on my own, come up with conversations, sound intelligent, and try not to look like I was frightened to death. My initial reaction was to say no and to stay within that comfort zone I knew so well, but I knew I had to say yes. If I couldn't go to a social event with a group of women, how in the world would I continue to go to meetings and events with clients and business owners? I swallowed hard and said yes.

The event was enjoyable, and the women were friendly and welcoming. I came home with a renewed sense of optimism that I might be able to pull this off—whatever "this" was. Accepting the invitation was an instance where the saying "You never know when one small incident can change the course of a life" would be true. WBN certainly changed mine.

I ultimately experienced tremendous growth through WBN, where I began to find my voice and my confidence over the next few years. I became treasurer and then president. With a board of nine women and close to one hundred members, it brought out leadership qualities that I had used in our business but never acknowledged. My confidence continued to grow as I realized how much I enjoyed interacting with and leading this group of women and, honestly, how good I was at it.

Through WBN, I met and worked with a life coach who helped me develop my confidence and work through the emotional journey of the loss of Sam. I met two future business partners. I participated in Leadership Frederick County, a program of the local Chamber of Commerce. This is also where I found my love of speaking in front of a group. It was hard to reconcile who I used to be—shy, not willing to be noticed—with someone who loved being in front of a room full of people and speaking into a microphone! But there I was, looking forward to and enjoying being front and center.

Much of who I am today is because of WBN, and I will be eternally grateful for the initial invitation that led me there. Never underestimate the power of connection!

Turning Points

"So, what *do* you know?" This question, again and again from my life coach, came in response to my consistent "I don't know!" answer to almost every question I faced. My answer allowed me not to have the responsibility of knowing or of having to act on that knowledge. Eventually, she helped me see that even if I didn't know the entire answer, I at least knew *something* and could start from there, then take the next step, then the next. My automatic response of "I don't know" was me playing small.

Another way of sabotaging myself was to constantly say—and believe—"I don't have a choice!" It was a constant refrain I had used with Sam whenever I felt obligated to do something I didn't want to, which allowed me to feel resentful that I couldn't do what *I* wanted. Deep in my heart, I knew I'd never take that step anyway. But this way, I could blame it on someone else. My perspective changed when my life coach helped me rephrase it to, "The choice I'm making is." What a life-changer! As I began taking responsibility for my choices, my confidence began to grow. This budding confidence made playing small feel uncomfortable, and I was opening myself up to new opportunities, but I still had setbacks.

Having a life coach during that time allowed me to work through my despair and grief faster and helped me to begin believing in myself. I never had the courage or confidence to take responsibility for my life and choices. Now that I had to, my coach showed me what I was truly capable of doing. I had it in me to direct my own destiny and make decisions for myself instead of relying on others to make them for me.

One of those decisions was to become a life coach myself. The training helped me realize that I was the only one who could control my actions and reactions. Blaming others for my circumstances only kept me mired in them. It wasn't until I started to take responsibility for my choices and attitude that I began to climb out of my self-imposed aura of "not good enough" and see real change in myself and my interactions with others. This realization helped me grow my confidence and recognize that I had gifts to share with others.

I used to repeat to myself after Sam's death, "It is what it is." It was a way of accepting what was happening and learning to live with it. Then one day, I learned that there was another part to this saying: "But it will be what you make of it." I knew instinctively that although I wasn't able to fully embrace and believe that second part just yet, when I truly believed it, I would have turned a corner. And I did! I realized that my outlook on any situation reflected my attitude, rather than the other way around. This was a revelation for me. I remind myself of this when I encounter obstacles, even today. It's crucial to remember that my life is a direct reflection of my attitude.

Friends

I don't know what I would have done without my best friend, Joyce. She called me multiple times each week, checking on me and making sure I was okay. She knew I was working myself to the point of exhaustion and did her best to provide me relief from my worries. She had me over for dinner often, a birthday get-together, and other outings that meant the world to me. Without her, I would have been lost. Knowing she was a phone call away at any time was a godsend.

It was harder for most other people to know how to interact with me. My first Father's Day without my father or Sam is one example. I didn't know how I was going to survive the day. I knew I needed to be strong for my daughters, that they would be feeling the pain as much as I was. As the day wore on and I heard only from my mom, the girls, and one friend, I spiraled deeper and deeper into the anxiety that I struggled to keep at bay on a good day. How could no one know what a terrible day it was for me? Why was no one else thinking of me being alone and dealing with my emotions?

When I later told a few friends and family how upset I was that they didn't call me, some responded that they didn't want to "upset" me by reminding me of what I'd lost. Another friend didn't know what to say, which kept her from reaching out. That's when I began to realize people's complicated reactions toward the grief and suffering of others. They don't know what to say, so they stay silent.

Being the social initiator had always been difficult for me, so the friends who said "Call me if you need anything" started fading away. I barely had the energy to take care of myself, so calling someone to ask for help was often beyond my capabilities. I eventually began cultivating new friends, and, as a result of my experience, I am more conscious about reaching out to someone who might be struggling. Sometimes, it is hard and I might not know what to say. But I've found that a simple "I thought of you and wanted to let you know" is a great place to start and will likely mean more to them than I'll ever know.

Worrying About Finances

Since Shannon was living with me for the year after college while waiting to get accepted into grad school, she often bore the brunt of my anxiety.

"I hate your goddam father," I sobbed to Shannon as I poured myself a glass of wine, then returned to a bunch of papers. Financial statements, income statements, payroll reports, mortgage payments, and bills. I glanced at my budget software and then back down at the bank statements.

"I just don't know what I'm going to do! Why couldn't he have left me with more? It was his FUCKING JOB to do financial planning. He always did it for everyone else—his clients, friends, hell, random people on the street. But when it came to his family . . . he just never took the time. He always left it to later. His work and everyone else always came first. His life insurance—that hadn't been updated since we got married. Why couldn't we have sat down for fifteen minutes and gotten a better one? With the business, this house . . . it was absolutely necessary to do. But he just never got around to doing it. Too busy taking care of everyone else. How could he do this to me? I don't know what to do!" My emotions, coupled with all of my worries, were spiraling out of control.

"Mom, I understand your anger," responded Shannon. "Dad often did take care of other people before his family. All of those clients, community members, and friends who came to pay their last respects at his viewing. He had helped them all in some way, but he often left doing things around the house or for his family to the last minute or forgot completely. But we need to figure out what to do. Crying over financial statements every night isn't productive. You must figure out how to put yourself out there and get clients."

I knew that Shannon felt my fears were overblown, and perhaps they were. But it was hard to see through the fog of grief when I was looking at the dwindling money available for the future. The life insurance was a fraction of what was needed for our current lifestyle. A good portion of our household income from the accounting business was now going to pay the new CPA. In addition, we had lost a few good clients.

Convincing people that they needed our services in the middle of an economic recession was difficult enough. Giving them a good reason to pay us money was hard while their own businesses were crumbling around them.

Shannon and I looked over the numbers together. I had already cut back on a lot, but losing more than half of my income while increasing my expenses due to the loss of a spouse seemed like an insurmountable mountain to climb. Why, oh why hadn't Sam and I planned better? I knew I would struggle financially without him, but it was never important enough to do anything about. We always had tomorrow, right? WRONG!

If I was honest with myself, a small part of me didn't want to make it. In some ways, it would have been easier. The business could fail, and I could say, "Oops, I tried." No more worrying over clients, employees, debt, and everything else. I could retreat into a smaller house, find a job to cover the necessities, and spend the rest of my time as a hermit, wallowing in self-pity. What if I did make the business profitable? I would have to continue, every day, with that responsibility. Every day, I would have to be brave, together, and powerful. Sometimes, it was too much to think about, so I continued to see failure.

But other days, I knew I had come too far at this point to give up. A part of me was growing, expanding, and seeing my potential. A small voice was gradually getting louder, telling me that I had relevance and was important, not just to others but also to myself.

"Shannon, I'm sorry," I said as we finished. "Please, don't think I'm mad at your father. I think it's the 'anger stage' of grief, or whatever it's called. I worry about what to do. I do know, sometimes, that I should be grateful. Having to work helps me not think about how much I miss your dad. If he had left me tons of money, I could skate through these problems and have nothing to do but twiddle my thumbs and cry. It would have been nice if he could have left me just a little bit more. Yes, that would have helped a lot. I guess also it's good to have other problems to think about besides how much I miss that man. That loving, distracted, pain-in-the-ass man." I smiled through my tears.

The Holidays

I was determined that we would not spend Christmas at home, which would have meant following the same routine we did every year, but devastated that Sam wasn't there. My solution was for the girls and me to go to my brother's place in Oregon, where we could experience our emotions without Sam's mom or my mom to witness and participate in our misery. We could visit Ken and Paula's new home and forgo the ritual that was our typical Christmas. The trip ended up being unsettling with my brother but a bonding experience with my girls.

Christmas Day turned out to be a good one. Spending time with Ken and Paula, without expectations of a schedule or particular type of interactions, made the day relaxing. We opened gifts, ate delicious meals and snacks, and talked about random things. For the most part, we could hold our grief at bay.

The next day was a different story.

We had taken a day trip to Seattle. Coming home, Ken got lost and, in his frustration, lost his temper. Paula took over driving, angrily hunched over the steering wheel while he sat in the passenger seat in huffy silence. I started crying, the discord sending me over the edge while the girls sat in uncomfortable silence in the back. It was a long two hours back home.

When we returned to the house, Ken stormed upstairs, and the girls started looking for alcohol. One of them turned on some loud music, and we started dancing. At one point, a joint was passed around, and the girls seemed impressed that not only did I not discourage it, I also partook of it. I was feeling wild and free and somewhat reckless. Ken eventually joined us, having slept off his anger. Paula had joined in with our crazy antics and saw a side of us rarely seen.

While we may vaguely remember the bad parts, what we took away was a time when we all let loose, had a great time, and danced our grief away. There was also a subtle recognition that, had Sam been there, we would not have had that experience. Not only would we not have had the grief that pulled us together, but we also would not have been so bold as to smoke a joint in front of him. We were thousands of miles from home, taking another step in our lives. As we did, we also left him further behind. While we missed him immensely and would have given anything to have him back, we were also beginning to recognize the power of bonding with each other as we stumbled into the future without him there to fix everything for us.

Conversations with Shannon

Having Shannon around was a blessing in that first year. Even though our schedules didn't overlap often—I worked during the day at the office, and she worked evenings at a restaurant—just having her presence in the house was calming. It also gave us an opportunity for conversations, most of which centered around my worries about the business.

When I chastised her for her lack of motivation for networking and applying for jobs, she reminded me that I was just as scared of networking as she was. We often giggled about the ridiculous things we did to avoid calling people or answering phones. Sometimes, I didn't understand how we functioned in this world with our terror of phones, but somehow we managed. One conversation had me relaying my story of fixing the main bathroom toilet, not wanting to call the plumber.

"Ahh," she said, thinking about living in a rented house during college, "this is why I miss having a landlord!"

"This is why I miss having a husband," I replied pointedly.

We made eye contact and then burst into tears. Landlords were attached to the property you were renting. But husbands . . . I missed the man who was right there, on call, ready to improvise the shit out of fixing a problem. Sometimes his solutions were efficient, sometimes not. But he always had one up his sleeve.

Yet another evening, a few weeks later, we were drinking, laughing, and joking, and she was (lovingly) yelling at me for my self-defeatist attitude. I was talking about my struggles, looking more for sympathy than encouragement. She got annoyed by my attitude and took the list of goals I'd recently written, crumpled them up, threw them on the ground, and stomped on them.

"There, fine! Look! There are your dreams! How do you feel now?" she yelled.

"I don't know," I replied. Then, breaking into a grin, I responded, "Tipsy! This wine is delicious!" And back to laughter we went.

I wasn't sure what I was going to do when Shannon was no longer there. In addition to our interactions, she also went grocery shopping and cooked our dinners—something Sam had always done and I was not fond of doing. When I mentioned this to her, she suggested I find another husband, one who could cook and fix things around the house.

I shook my head, grinning. "I can't have that! My closet is full. I love having the whole thing for myself. I don't even have to put all of my off-season clothes away. It's delightful. If I married, I'd have to give up all that space."

"Well, we'll just have to figure out another solution," she responded, grinning.

The conversations with Shannon throughout that year were crazy. One minute we were shaking with laughter, the next with tears. We seemed bound by these extreme emotions. Being unable to have a normal conversation made those evenings both draining and delightful. I loved spending these times with Shannon, trying to figure things out together. But we were always on the edge of despair, and it was so easy to slip.

The First Anniversary

I was gearing up for the anniversary date, Tuesday, April 12, to be the difficult day. However, I was not prepared for my visceral reaction on Monday morning. I didn't realize that *that* would be the day I felt deep in my heart and gut, remembering that a year ago, I spent a lovely weekend with Sam, kissed him goodbye on Monday morning, and never saw him alive again. I felt myself falling into grief, despair, and total helplessness as I relived that morning and the never-ending anxiety that had been with me since. I felt like I had been drowning all year, feverishly dogpaddling to keep myself afloat. That morning, I wasn't sure if I had the strength or energy to continue.

I went into the office but could not stop crying. I do not like others to see my weakness, but I could not contain it. As I had learned over the past year, the longer I was around people, the better I could control my emotions, and it was the same for that day. By the afternoon, I had myself under control and able to function enough to make it through the next few days to the deadline on the 15th. I knew I had passed a milestone and survived. Maybe there was hope for the future.

The Dating Scene

"Live for today, for you never know what tomorrow will bring," I told Shannon. It was the end of April. I'd made it through the year after Sam's death, tax season was over, and I felt some of the burden lifted from my shoulders, if only for a bit. I felt more freedom to try to figure out what I wanted my future to be. I had joined a dating website and had conversations with men. But the guilt! Oh, my, the guilt. My husband had only been dead a year. How could I be thinking about dating someone else?

I knew I loved Sam and that I would until the day I died. But I also knew that he was gone forever. I loved being married, with the companionship, sharing, and love it brought. At first, my reaction was that I'd remain single, date a lot of different men, and have the time of my life. But the reality for me was the time of my life meant sharing it with someone I loved. Hence, the dating site. *Do I dare think it could happen again?*

This was my mindset as I began conversations with a few men on the website. The first time I met one for coffee, I drove around the parking lot three times before finally pulling into a spot. It was one of the scariest things I've ever done.

Then, I started conversing with Bob. Emails back and forth, talking about our interests, likes, and dislikes, and getting to know each other as much as possible via email. Bob took his camera to work and had a coworker take his picture so he could upload it to his profile to contact me. Oh, the beginnings of a romance!

After several emails, we agreed to talk via phone. It was the Friday of Memorial Day weekend, and we had talked for a few hours when he said, "My daughter's calling me, and I really need to talk to her." Evidently, I was enjoying the conversation so much that I said, "That's fine. You can call me when you're done if you want to continue our conversation." He did, but he still gives me a hard time about it today because he said I didn't want to get off the phone.

Bob and I met for the first of many dates, and the conversation continued. It was a challenge to admit that I could date someone seriously just over a year after Sam's death. I wasn't feeling comfortable about people knowing I was dating someone. I imagined them saying, "How could she profess to love Sam so much but date someone else so soon?" The reality was that people were very supportive of my dating, and many said that it inspired them to see me happy again.

With Bob, I felt such a connection, and I felt so much caring. Maybe, just maybe, this was okay. But how would my girls feel about it? I knew they were poised to begin their adult life, but how would they feel about me seriously dating someone so soon after their dad's death? Would it feel like a betrayal? As usual, Shannon put it in good perspective for me.

"You know, I'm just not sure if this is supposed to happen twice," I told Shannon, referring to my relationship with Bob. "I already had this once. A new love; that beginning, when it's new and fresh and fun, but you're ready for it to last forever. I had a great life and marriage. I know of other women whose relationship hasn't been good for one reason or another, or they are unable to find a new partner. Who am I to deserve the chance for another good man in my life?"

"Mom," said Shannon emphatically. "Who are you to have that? But then again, who are you to have your husband stolen away after only twenty-five years? You've lost a father and a husband just six months apart, then turn around and wonder if you deserve anything else good in your life. I don't think it has anything to do with what you deserve. Other women didn't deserve their lot in life, yet some jerks gave them that. You can't ask if you deserve it; it's just what is."

"You know," she continued, "there's this quote I remember: 'Life isn't about making good choices to get good things. It's about admitting what you want and not being afraid to go after it.'"

I snapped my head up. "You know," I said, "that's exactly . . . I need to write that down. That would be a really good quote for the motivational speeches I want to give someday. Can you say that again?"

She repeated it for me. Then I asked, "Where did you get that from?"

She smiled fiendishly. "*Weeds*. You know, that show I've told you about. Where the husband suddenly dies—from a heart attack—and then the wife decides to make an income by selling weed in the suburbs. Like I've said before, that's a good money-maker if you're really concerned about money!"

"Ha, ha," I said, shaking my head in exasperation.

The Motivational Speech

"Mom!" Shannon said, in that annoyed voice she used when I was being difficult. "You *say* you want to be a motivational speaker. You *say* you want to make a difference in people's lives, especially women. You want to show them that they have it in them to overcome challenges, even if they don't believe it at first. If that's true, then your speech cannot be, 'I started to become strong after my husband died, but it was too hard, so I quit!'"

Such wisdom from my oldest. I wanted to scold her, but I knew she was right. I had been asked to speak at the Maryland Women's Conference in Frederick in November 2011. I really wanted to do it, which surprised me—I would have never considered even going to an event like this, let alone being a speaker at one. In front of a bunch of people? What had I gotten myself into? I let the fear sink into me, and the doubts started. I would then convince myself that I'd never be able to do this, which is what I'd told Shannon, and hence her response.

The truth was, I was having difficulty reconciling my desire to give this speech with whom I had always known myself to be. But I couldn't deny the pull I felt when I thought about doing it—the pull to show women that yes, they can survive, grow, and move forward after a devastating event. That they have the ability to control their destination, regardless of what life throws their way.

I entitled the speech "Developing a Winning Attitude: When Change = Opportunity." The standing-room-only audience was the largest of any speakers at the conference. I told my journey from owning a dairy farm to owning an accounting firm, from happily married to widowhood, and from shy to (mostly) confident. I fumbled a few times and shed a few tears, but it felt right, and it felt good. It was exactly what I needed to show my transition from feeling unimportant to inspiring other women with my experience. Afterward, people told me what a powerful speech it was and that it really inspired them. Mission accomplished for both them and me.

Lessons Learned

I was devastated. My friend Susan was in hospice. Her extended family had been called to say goodbye. She had fought hard this past year to overcome her cancer, but in the end, she was still defeated. Was there ever an end to the suffering? She was fifty-four.

I called my girls, saying, "I'm beyond sad about Susan. What does this say about faith, love, and healing energy? All the things we want to believe in, but how powerful are they, really? At the end of the day, we are still subject to the sucky rules of the universe—it's your turn to die." I was reliving Sam's death, the too-early loss of a good person who positively impacted everyone around him, just like Susan. Why did this keep happening?

"Bob has been a godsend to me tonight, comforting me," I continued. "I keep thinking how different my life would be if Sam had lived, but how much I love my life now. It's such a disconnect for me. I don't usually think about it, but Susan's death has brought it all to the forefront. I feel blessed for my life and what I have. But I'm also sad for what has been lost."

I realized that some of my disconnect was loving the life I had now, but one that did not include Sam. Yes, I would have loved to have grown old with him. But would I go back if I could? After knowing what was on the other side, life without him, could I give it all up? Would the girls? Because despite all of the pain, there were good things too. We changed. We grew. We women bonded together to survive. We found things to fill the big, gaping hole he left behind.

"Aw, Mom, I'm so sorry!" Jessica said. "Of course, these situations will bring up a lot of emotions and memories, and it's okay to feel them and be sad! And yes, at the end of the day, we cannot control the universe, but we can still do our best, be our best, and be positive." She paused. "I'm glad Bob is there for you. And yes, it seems weird, but it's two different yet connected parts of your life. And they're both equally important and beautiful!"

"I'm really sorry, Mom," said Danielle. "I know this is tough. But I think when it comes to faith, hope, love—we can't expect those things to stop something bad from happening. Those are the things that make the life we *do* have worth living, no matter how long or short that life may be."

"I'm glad Bob is there to comfort you," she continued. "I don't think there's anything wrong with wondering what your life might have looked like if it had gone how you'd expected. But it doesn't diminish what you love about your life now, just like loving your life now doesn't diminish the good times and loving memories you had with Dad before. At the end of the day, you can't change the past; you can only live in the present, look toward the future, and hope you make the world a little bit better."

My girls' responses said everything I needed to hear—not only comforting me but also giving me the realization that they had also grown and blossomed after Sam's death. They had learned a life lesson at an early age and used it to grow and spread their wisdom to others.

In the Future

"I love my life," I think often to myself nowadays. It's been almost fifteen years since Sam's death, and I've changed and accomplished a lot. I've married Bob, a wonderful man, with whom came another son and daughter, their spouses, and seven grandkids who have welcomed me into their families. I continued, merged, unmerged, sold, and retired from the accounting business in the seven years after Sam's death. I have written and published two books and co-owned two other businesses. I have an active social life, enjoy public speaking and community activities, and travel often. It's a perfect life for me. But it's different than my life would have been if Sam were still alive. And I am a different person.

I've often said that while he was alive, Sam tried to gently push and pull me out of my comfort zone, but I wouldn't have it. By his death, he catapulted me out of it to become the woman he always knew I was, but was hidden—confident in myself and my abilities. His death forced me to stand up for myself and take responsibility for my life and actions. It brought my girls and me, as well as my mother and me, much closer as we learned to recognize our talents and abilities and depend on each other for support.

Thank you, Sam, for the wisdom you imparted while with us and the lessons you helped us learn after your death. You will always be with us, encouraging us to continue to move forward, be and do our best, and lean on each other for strength. We will always love you and hold you close in our hearts. Without your untimely departure, we would not be the women we are now. While we can never get that marvelous man back, we can also never return to the women we were before his death. That was his final gift to us.

◘   ◘   ◘

John and Karen at their nephew's wedding, 2008

Short Karen's Story

That September Afternoon

I watched as he stepped back into the hospital waiting room. There was worry, fear, and pasted-on strength in his face. As I stood, his eyes directed me to a private corner by the window. Not seeking my hand or my touch, my husband said, "I have pancreatic cancer."

We stood there in the hospital lobby, just looking at each other. I took a deep breath. My husband, head of operations for a small company and ever the responsible one, pulled out his cell phone and called his boss.

"Bob, you know we've talked about your needing a succession plan in case you get hit by a bus? Well, I just got hit by a bus. We need to make some plans for that, too."

As he talked, my mind started racing. My husband had one of the worst cancers there is. I felt like I'd been kicked in the gut. My heart seemed to stop. What do we need to do to get rid of this cancer? How do we start? How do I help him face this horrid news? What can I do to ease his fears? How do I get this man of mine to talk about his worries? He has always kept his thoughts and feelings so close to his chest.

Then, my brain began problem solving. How much time do we have? What do we need to do in case he doesn't get better? What if we can't get it done in time? Who do we need to talk with? What should we do first? Where do we start? We needed to make some significant plans. I needed to take a very deep breath.

One thing we had going for us was our experience with planning. John had been an Army officer for thirty-one years. We had moved fifteen times during his career to seven states and two foreign countries as he changed jobs. Most of the planning about what to take to each new post was managed jointly. However, I was responsible for managing the packing and reestablishing our lives in each new location. Even the winnowing down of pantry and freezer items needed planning. With each move, I also had the task of finding new job opportunities for myself. I was skilled with the monumental and the minor.

We were an excellent team for changes and transitions. This one was different. Quite different.

Here and There in Childhood

As the daughter of a skilled telephone technician during the industry's significant operational changes, I was subjected to constant change. When my father completed the "changeover" of one regional company's equipment, we moved on to the next. Before I met John, I had already experienced years of disruptions. I moved six times before I turned ten. Every move meant a change in schools for my younger sister and me. By fifth grade, I was in my seventh home and my seventh new school.

Finally, with my father in a more permanent position, my parents bought a house. My sister, Cindy, and I had our own rooms. After six other schools, that seventh school promised stability, a gift for my short life of continual instability. I could relax in the security of a permanent home instead of the childhood stress I had been experiencing.

Near the end of sixth grade, I turned twelve and had my first slumber party for my birthday. My friends and I had the basement "rec room" all to ourselves for the entire night. We laughed, ate, talked about attending junior high the following year, and slept a little. It was so great. I basked in the camaraderie of this new permanent circle of friends.

After my friends left the next morning, my mother told me my father had been promoted. We were going to move. My world slid out from under me. I'm not sure if the tears came from disappointment or anger. I was fed up with all the disruptions to stability and angry that I had to leave friends and familiarity behind again.

During a childhood full of changes and losses, I experienced sadness, disappointment, and disruption with each move. My response to the news from my mother that morning was all of those. I may not have been able to collectively label those emotions, but they had the same characteristics as grief. They were significant and intense. My expectations for keeping those friendships and sharing them through more years of school ended that morning.

However, Cindy and I were blessed that the small town we moved to provided an opportunity to make new friends. Our new next-door neighbor was Reverend Pierce, the pastor of one of the churches in town. At his invitation, my mother wisely enrolled my sister and me in the summer Bible school program. We made new friends in small groups, which made it easier for us to transition into the school classroom that fall.

The Pierces became family friends, and that friendship remains today, sixty years later. We stayed in that town for six years. It was a great place to finish my childhood. I made good friends and was active in the school, church, 4-H, and band. I finally had the stable, engaging, settled life that I craved.

However, eight days after my high school graduation, we followed a moving van out of town and to another new home. I grieved again about leaving my friends and missing out on shared experiences during my college breaks. Permanent separation is a different kind of loss than death, but it can still cause grief.

The First Transformational Changes

On my third weekend as a freshman in college, I met John. It was a blind date on a Sunday night when the dorm cafeteria was closed. I accepted because it was a free meal, but it turned out to be more than that.

I began to build my college life around him and his activities. In many ways, most of my college life was wrapped around him. I did not recognize what I was missing. I loved being with others but failed to build long-term friendships or relationships with anyone outside the circle I shared with him. That has been a lifetime disappointment.

When we finished college, John and I had no plans for marriage. That wasn't quite the finish I expected, but uncertainty was in the air. The Vietnam War was still raging. John was drafted into military service. I took a short-term research job in Appalachia. By this time, my family had moved to Michigan.

I went to Michigan to pack up whatever I needed for the summer, my temporary job, and the beginning of my "grown-up" life. I had three or four days to get ready. My sister Cindy was still at college, so we didn't get to visit.

My mother had gone to work the day I was leaving, so I said goodbye to her early in the morning. Dad waited while I finished cleaning my room, joined me for breakfast, and helped me load my summer suitcases into the car. He was unusually attentive and present. As I was getting ready to pull out of the driveway, he leaned into the car window and said, "Karen, how would you and your sister feel if your mother and I went our separate ways?" I was speechless.

We talked for a few minutes, but I couldn't think of anything wise to say. I remember thinking, *I'm moving on with the rest of my life, but what about Cindy?* I couldn't speak for her. I thought, *Does my mother know?* Probably not. If she had known, my visit would have been much different. There would have been turmoil or tears. Once Dad announced he was leaving, he would probably do so immediately. I must have been the reason for the delay. He wanted to tell me before I moved on with my life. I have no idea how my sister found out. I don't know how or when he told my mother.

As I drove away, I thought about always being Dad's favorite and connected to him. I should have recognized his unusual behavior. I should have known something wasn't quite right. If I'd noticed, we might have had more time to discuss his decision. I might have gotten answers to questions I never got to ask. I could have asked why, but I wouldn't have gotten an answer any different than that he wasn't happy and the relationship wasn't working. I had observed that for years.

I had no idea what would happen at home that evening, that week, when or how. He surprised me at such an inopportune time that I hadn't even thought of those questions until I was miles down the road.

I had to drive 450 miles and arrive ready for my new job the next day. I was out of touch with my family while they were going through changes I didn't know about. In 1969, cell phones, emails, texts, or any of today's easy communication options did not exist. We had no easy way of keeping in touch, and I truthfully didn't know what to do.

I was afraid to call home on Father's Day. If Dad had already left, I didn't want to hurt Mom. I didn't know where he was or how to reach him. No one was calling me. The research job kept our team moving from town to town. My family knew how to contact me in an emergency, but the constant communication parents and children have today with cell phones differs from the era of payphones and long-distance charges.

What a strange summer that was. I had left the nest like many college students, but my nest was falling out of the tree anyway.

Everything had changed. My family. My job. My life. This seismic family shift was another step propelling me toward the self-sufficiency and independence that I would come to rely on through other changes in my life.

I spent my summer traveling with a team as part of a U.S. Senate-designated dietary health survey in Appalachia. We moved every few days and lived in motels in one town or another. My unsettled summer had one calming aspect—occasional visits from John before he reported to Army basic training.

In late August 1969, I was offered a position as a consumer economics teacher in a newly integrated high school in central Florida. I drove back to Michigan, where the house was in disarray, and only my mother was home. In two days, I packed a car full of boxes and suitcases with all my possessions and began my twelve-hundred-mile drive to Bartow, Florida.

I had a new role and an unfamiliar curriculum, while the students had to adjust to a new environment and develop new relationships in the integrated setting. The classroom presented significant changes for each of us.

For the spring semester, I was scheduled to teach sex education. As a young, single woman, I was not looking forward to teaching the subject to students only a few years younger than me. The first semester was full of new learning. In the second semester, I would have to learn how to balance subject matter with embarrassment and teenage humor.

But first, Christmas vacation.

I flew back to Michigan to spend Christmas with my mother and sister. The year had been turmoil for all of us and we seemed quite content to ignore any discussion of the difficulties. I have no memories of the holidays that year until the last few days when I flew to West Virginia.

John was home on leave. He met me at the airport gate and carried my suitcase to the car. When we got in, he started the car and then pulled a large box out of the back seat. When I unwrapped the box, I discovered a pile of bath towels. "Dig down," he said.

Deep inside the folds of the towels, I found a much smaller box. Inside was an engagement ring. His proposal was in the front seat of a car in a cold airport parking lot with a box full of bath towels. Although it wasn't delivered from his knees and there was no romantic music, dinner, or flowers. I still said, "Yes." Forever into the future, I would tease him by saying, "You know, I only said 'yes' so I wouldn't have to teach sex education that next semester."

We spent the next three or four days rapidly planning the wedding for a date less than a month away. We had to fit it into a short window between his Army training commitments. Reverend Pierce and his wife were now living near John's family. Since my family had recently fallen apart and was miles away, the Pierces made the wedding happen.

John returned to training, and I returned to Florida to tender my resignation and finish the first semester. I then packed everything I owned again and drove north.

Becoming a Soldier's Wife

We were married at two o'clock on Saturday. At four o'clock on Sunday, he kissed me goodbye and flew back to training camp in Missouri. I moved in with my in-laws. It was an emotional weekend of celebration and loss. For the next thirty-one years, the Army would be the principal change agent in my life. In my childhood, I could never have imagined how all those changes prepared me for the life I would lead.

Three weeks after the wedding, John called me just after lunch on a Friday afternoon. "Pack your car with whatever you're going to need for the next six months, and be ready to leave tomorrow," he said.

He was in Missouri. I was in West Virginia. Before midnight the next night, he was required to be inside the gates of Fort Belvoir, Virginia, just south of Washington, D.C. Through the strength and will of twenty-two-year-olds, we managed to make it happen. He signed in at the gate at 11:55 p.m. and was whisked to the barracks.

At midnight on a cold February night, I was a new bride alone at the gate to Fort Belvoir. Becoming an independent Army wife started that night. The scene was totally dark, totally foreign, and totally scary! However, the Pierces had stepped in again and given me the name of a former high school classmate who lived in Washington. After navigating through the city in the middle of the night, a couch was waiting for me in her apartment on the city's north side.

Early the next day, I went to the housing office at the Army post, as John had suggested. He told me they could help me find a safe place to live. After I signed in, a young man approached me and said, "Hi. I'm Vince. I heard you give your name. Are you John Justice's new wife?" He introduced himself and then his wife, Judy. Vince had met John in the training group in Missouri and was starting class at Belvoir a week later. Judy and I became roommates for the next six months.

John and Vince were in Officer Candidate School and would live in the barracks with other soldiers, isolated from families and distractions. After our frantic drive to Fort Belvoir's gate, I only saw John at church on Sunday mornings and Wednesday nights for the first six months of our marriage. For me, that honeymoon most brides dream of didn't happen.

Soldiering On

John completed Officer Candidate School in late July 1970. With a small U-Haul trailer behind us, we headed north for a ten-week training session in Massachusetts. By Thanksgiving, we were living in Augsburg, Germany. By Easter 1971, we were in Worms, Germany.

I taught in an American nursery school in Germany for a couple of years. Then, we moved to Texas. During my four years there, I worked in a standard daycare center before I was given a fantastic new opportunity. I was hired to initiate and manage a daycare center that would serve as a child development lab for the high school child development course. Before leaving Texas, I helped edit childcare center staff training materials.

We moved to Arizona in October and to Alaska the following May. I managed a daycare center for a church in Alaska for three years. Just before we left Alaska in 1981, I met the owner of a new company called Discovery Toys. I signed up as a sales rep, left all my early childhood teaching materials behind, and took the new early childhood education product catalogs on our move to New England.

We were only in New England for ten months. I discovered that working in direct, home-based sales wasn't a good fit for my very mobile life. My short experience in sales, however, was enough to help me land a job selling direct mail ads when we moved to Maryland. It's a stretch to find a connection between early childhood education, selling educational toys, and selling advertising to business owners. However, my new boss believed that teachers made good sales representatives.

With that sales job, I also discovered a new love: the business world. I was good at that job. I loved it. I got involved in a saleswoman's organization. I was making a significant income compared to my previous earnings. I was feeling successful, satisfied, and happy. But, six years after arriving in Maryland, the Army decided John's career growth required another move. I had to leave that dream job behind. We were moving from the metropolitan area of Washington, D.C. to a small town in the middle of Texas. I cried at the drop of a hat on the way there and for several weeks after that.

However, I learned to accept the unchangeable and make the most of what I had. I experienced a positive change in that small Texas town. I took a job with the Chamber of Commerce and loved the organizational management and involvement with the business community.

Transitions, especially without specific professional expertise, require adaptation, creativity, flexibility, and an open mind. They're not easy. These skills were valuable in determining what I could and would do in each new location. They also were to become beneficial to me as a widow. They helped me adjust, solve problems, and deal with all the additional life changes.

After a regular three-year assignment in Texas, more adapting, flexibility, and creativity were required. John was offered a job working with NATO, the North Atlantic Treaty Organization, in Oslo, Norway. As with most assignments, when he had a choice, he discussed the options with me.

"Would you like to go to Norway?" he asked me.

"Why not?" I answered.

The University of Maryland usually provided civilian educational opportunities wherever military members were assigned. I assumed I could further my career by earning a graduate degree in business while we were in Oslo. As soon as the last moving box was emptied and everything was put in its new place, I was off to the education office to talk with the University of Maryland representative.

In my short meeting with her, I discovered the University of Maryland did not offer an MBA program in our location. There weren't even any classes that could be used for a graduate degree. Unfortunately, in 1991, there were no Google searches that could have provided that information for me in advance.

I walked out of the education office feeling empty. I was again faced with bitter disappointment and a total disruption to my expectations and plans. I stood in the hallway next to their door with tears running down my cheeks.

When I looked up, I noticed a bulletin board beside me. In the lower right corner was a small four-by-four-inch ad promoting an MBA program taught in English at BI Norwegian Business School, one of

Europe's twenty best business colleges. The angel and serendipity, who sit on each of my shoulders, came through. They have saved me and opened doors for me all my life.

I managed to survive graduate school twenty-three years after earning my undergraduate degree. In addition to my studies, I paid attention to friendships this time. Unlike when I was an undergrad, I began to realize how important my own friends were. Since I'd left my high school friends behind, I had made only two long-lasting friendships. During graduate school in Norway, I made two new very dear friends: Isabelle from France and Ayfer from Turkey. Isabelle reappeared at a critical time in my future. I also became friends with the wife of a Scottish officer who was serving with John. We've all remained friends since then.

Preparing to Change Hats

When we left Norway and returned to the Washington, D.C. area for new jobs, I encountered a different challenge in my job search. Despite holding a Master of Business Administration degree, it was from a foreign school. Although I wanted to work in international business, I lacked the professional network to assist me in transitioning to that field. Instead, I combined my MBA with a different part of my education: a lifetime of planning travel wherever we had lived. I became the director of tourism promotion for a county in Maryland. I followed that with a combination of tourism and education and did workforce training across the state for several years, including the unexpected aspect of writing and delivering training materials for taxicab drivers. I created training sessions on moving from the front line to a supervisory role and improving employee productivity.

As the end of John's thirty-one-year military career approached, we had decisions to make. We knew what we wanted for the next phase of our lives in general. As with most decisions I had made in life, I kept a crucial goal in mind based on what fit my inner being. John and I created a well-designed spreadsheet matrix. We did some investigative travel. Without knowing it at the time, the building we chose for our new home determined the community that would be my permanent home.

The northern border of Maryland met our requirements of a temperate climate, wooded mountains, and being on the same side of the country as our families. Our final decision was somewhat based on all the detailed elements of our matrix and made us smile with anticipation. However, we missed a few of the logical and practical details.

Just months before our fiftieth birthdays, John and I purchased a 13,000-square-foot powerhouse: a hundred-year-old industrial building. It still had two coal-fired boilers in the basement. The second floor had been an institutional laundry with arched-transom windows that had no glass in the window arches. Two apartments were on the top floor. The attic had a cupola that actually served as a vent for the coal-fired boilers. The rooms had old plaster walls, and there was a pit in front of the entry door. Our friends and family thought we'd lost our minds. We thought we'd found another adventure.

The building required lots of work to make it look like a residence instead of an institutional building. Life was always one project after the other, yet we loved it. We hosted celebration parties with family and friends. We enjoyed gorgeous weather and wildlife visits. We took lovely morning walks without ever leaving our own property. Yes, we loved it. The project was a bonding experience. We enjoyed the collective creativity.

A couple of years after we bought "the project," John retired. The Army was no longer responsible for the changes in our lives. John found civilian contractor jobs. I did consulting work for the state, small businesses, and nonprofits.

I was ready for greater involvement and connections in my local community. I was married to a busy introvert who could be social and was well liked but preferred to retreat behind the closed doors of our home.

We had moved somewhere permanently, and I wanted to start creating lasting friendships. In hindsight, that decision was one of my best.

I got involved. Many of the friendships I created are now twenty years old. Having friends for that long is a significant accomplishment in my changing life.

I eventually became president of the Women's Business Network of Frederick. Among the women in the organization, I developed several close friendships. A couple of years later, through that group, I met Karen Smith-Racicot, one of my coauthors.

As president of the group, I initiated a mentoring walk in the park. The event became successful and, although modified, is still held annually. Because of that event, I was recruited as the first program director of Woman to Woman Mentoring, a program for eighteen- to twenty-eight-year-old women in our area. I *loved* that job, yet . . .

I decided to resign in 2011 for two reasons. One, my sister and I had recently moved our mother north from Florida to our area. Mom had been falling frequently and needed to be closer to us. We found an excellent progressive living location where support would be available twenty-four hours a day.

Secondly, John had changed hats again to that of operations officer for a small corporation. His job required lots of travel, sometimes for two or three weeks at a time. I wanted to go with him occasionally, so I traded my mentoring program job for not being alone for long stretches of time.

In 2011, I did not foresee how fortunate and well-timed my retirement decision was. It was only three years later that we stood in that hospital lobby facing the pancreatic cancer diagnosis. Leaving my mentoring program had filled me with regrets, but after his diagnosis, I was so very grateful I had made the tough decision to quit when I did.

I had suffered the grief of separations and departures all my life. They brought bitter disappointments, significant changes, and disruptions to my expectations and plans. However, the grief and changes that came with the pancreatic cancer diagnosis were a different experience—gut-wrenchingly different.

John is strong and seemingly healthy. How could this happen? I kept thinking. While I focused on managing the change John's eventual death would bring, my inner self was rocked with shock, dread, and fear.

Weaknesses

During the first year after John's diagnosis, I was determined to remain strong for two reasons. First, John was going to need my help and all the wisdom I could muster to support him through the treatments and the "transition." Managing a fatal illness has to be life's most introspective experience. Secondly, I wanted to demonstrate that I was going to be okay. I wanted him to understand that his concerns for my future were valid and important but that I could manage the drastic change. I tried to remain calm and confident.

I *was* confident that I would be okay. I knew I'd be secure to a sufficient degree. I knew that, whatever the circumstances, I could find a way to start over again. I'd done so all my life.

However, the calm part was hard. I tucked away the fears in pockets of my head and pulled off an Academy Award performance. Now and then, I'd cry my eyes out. Then, pull out the shroud that covered the pain.

If "fortunate" is a term one can use in the same sentence with pancreatic cancer, John was fortunate to have been diagnosed in an early stage of that cancer. We were also blessed that his boss Bob was John's good friend.

Bob was having lunch with his niece and her husband when John called about his diagnosis. Both lunch mates were doctors at major hospitals in Baltimore. One had worked with the top pancreatic surgeon at the Johns Hopkins Hospital. Thanks to this network of friends and their connections, John had surgery two weeks after diagnosis. The doctor told us a prognosis was impossible. He said John could have six months or fifteen years. Bad news. Good news.

While recognizing that we were always aware that life could end tomorrow, having a stated timeframe was unsettling. It shook our lives.

John started chemotherapy with all the ups and downs. He had one week of pain, discomfort, and weakness. The following week, he would continue to work a typical schedule and travel. I believe it was personally rewarding for John to have an excuse to spend time with his boss and friend Bob. I also enjoyed spending time with Bob and his wife Margaret. They had become good friends to both of us. Their support of John and then their ongoing support of me was exceptional and reassuring.

As time progressed, we began to make plans for his death and my survival and for maximizing the time left together. I planned a trip to Hawaii for John and me. He had always wanted to go. The airline and hotel points John had accumulated through all his work travel enabled me to acquire most of our flights and lodging virtually free. To add a bit of excitement to the trip without a lot of physical exertion, we took a flight over the Kilauea volcano that was erupting on the big island of Hawaii and then a helicopter ride on Kauai just before a Pacific hurricane arrived.

Meanwhile, my mother's health continued to fail and I became simultaneously needed by two loved ones. The decades of time I had expected to have with my husband had been shortened and I wanted to spend as many of my current hours with him as possible. Yet, my mother needed my attention, love, and support as her life was coming to an end. I didn't have as much time as I wanted with either of them. The constraints were emotionally draining.

Unleashing my emotions or talking with my nearest and dearest friends would have been the expected path of behavior. However, John was always reserved and private. I wanted to maintain a public impression of his strength. I feared putting a notch in the pedestal I thought he occupied in other people's minds. I didn't give our friends enough credit. I think I also didn't want to reveal *my* weakness. I feared that people would question my every mood or action, and be over-solicitous or critical.

Many people don't know how to help a widow. Sometimes it's equally difficult to know how to help someone whose spouse is terminally ill. Again, perhaps I didn't give my friends enough credit.

I found a sounding board in a very unusual place: a young man in Morocco. I'd met Jamal a few months before John's surgery. He was our guide on a tour of Morocco's wonderful highlights that I'd taken with a couple of friends in 2014.

For some reason, Jamal and I had a strong bond from the moment we met. I became his unofficial mentor. I also became a big sister, American mom, friend, and confidant. I listened to his worries about ailing family members and hurt feelings when he was betrayed by a friend. He became my unofficial counselor.

Jamal never met John, and that was a significant advantage. It was my private safe space. I could talk about anything I needed to express without fear, worry, or criticism. Thanks to the wonders of various tech platforms, we messaged, had video chats, and shared photos of our lives. He distracted me, listened, and offered sage advice for an unmarried man in his early thirties.

Not all of our communications involved my worries, concerns, complaints, or tears. I found the gender, generation, religious, cultural, economic, and educational differences fascinating. They provided us with a wide range of topics to discuss. The "escape" from my reality soothed me. However, one day I *did* call him in tears. I said, "Just let me cry. I need someone to be with me while I cry."

I had a friend who was a distant sounding board in multiple ways. That option was a unique gift.

Preparation for Widowhood

One of our first actions after John's surgery in October was to call a realtor. After sixteen years of working on the "project," we needed to sell our historic powerhouse and remove that responsibility as soon as possible. However, "possible" was seven months away, because our building and grounds were not appealing in the winter. Spring never arrived on our mountain until May, so we had a few months to get the building cleaned out.

We weren't piled to the rafters, but the building was huge. We lived on the two main levels and had filled those 5,200 square feet with furniture and décor. Of course, there were also some possessions we hadn't looked at in years, like John's stamp collection and hundreds of photographic slides from our early years together.

The 1,300-square-foot attic was full of Christmas décor, rolls of insulation, and boxes of forgotten items. The mostly industrial basement had tools galore, lawn and garden equipment, and supplies. Oh, so much stuff! All those earlier changes and moves after short residencies hadn't prepared me for what can accumulate over sixteen years in one place.

Some decisions were based on what John would never use again. However, I tried to be extremely sensitive about not removing his "life and loves" from what we took with us. While saving money on the move was important, I did not want to give *any* impression that I was erasing him from the future.

Preparing our unique home to sell was challenging. The industry has "rules" about removing clutter but removing "clutter" from that huge building was like taking away its personality. It was difficult to accomplish that task and still make the industrial building look as inviting as a home.

John and I hired my friend Tara, an interior designer, to help us "stage" our building before the sale. Fortunately, there was an excellent consignment shop in town that took many of the items Tara said should go away. Goodwill, Habitat for Humanity's ReStore, the Salvation Army, and other local charities benefited from many of our castoffs.

A month after John's surgery, two of his oldest friends came to visit. While we were driving around, we said, "Since you're a realtor, Nancy, let us show you one of the places we like in town. The neighborhoods are tightly packed but appealing."

On that serendipitous visit, we discovered new homes in that community were being built with backyards opening to the river and farmland beyond. We'd still have a viewscape similar to our rural powerhouse. The next day, we placed a down payment on one of the homes. It would be finished in a year. The challenge of a new home was settled.

As the days, weeks, and months rolled by, I started preparing myself for the inevitable. We needed to be sure all our legal information was in order. What about our financial planning? Where did that stand? What did I need to know?

My mind was working in various channels: financial, functional, housing, downsizing, loneliness, the absence of a spouse with a brilliant, clever mind . . . all the changes and losses I was going to be required to face.

As we planned for our inevitable future, familiarity, comfort, and confidence were extremely important to me. My good friend and lawyer Janice helped us review our wills to be sure everything was in order, that our intentions had not changed, and all details were accounted for.

John had previously become a life member of the Military Officers Association of America, which also provided assistance to surviving spouses. John told me that my first task after he passed was to call MOAA for help with the military financial paperwork and assistance in arranging the burial he preferred at Arlington National Cemetery.

We contacted our financial planner and told him our news. We had no idea what time frame we were working with, but together, the three of us looked at various scenarios, discussed my wishes and our possibilities, and then developed a plan. From then on, I became more involved in the conversations about decisions we were asked to make, and in reviewing the reports we received. I wanted to be sure I understood the information, and whether or not it was merely a point-in-time report or critical information.

We ensured that all bank accounts were joint. We also checked insurance policies, beneficiaries on retirement plans, and any other financial instruments we could think of.

All the arrangements, accounts, and other details that married people create and do as a couple were all going to be mine to manage. He was trying to finish big work projects in between chemo treatments. His energy went toward tasks he wanted to complete, so I picked up the household and family management tasks. I'd always managed my own bank account. Now I was managing our family accounts as well.

We made lists of his passwords so I could access or close his accounts and the joint ones he was managing. The one password we forgot was his cell phone. That mistake would later cost me money.

Three Losses, Back-to-Back

In September 2015, we were in California for John's job when my mother's caregivers called to tell me she had taken a turn for the worse. We caught a red-eye flight back across the country, and I was at my mother's side the next day.

Every day for a week, I'd drive to her care home. My sister had moved to Virginia the summer before John's diagnosis. She would have been there to support both Mom and me, but Cindy was also being torn between the duties of wife and daughter. Her husband had gone into a coma after heart surgery a few weeks before. She sat by *his* bedside for six weeks.

I spent a week with Mom mumbling in her drug-induced state and me talking about our family and our lives. One evening, I headed home earlier than usual. I could no longer bear the agony of suffering on her face. Not ten minutes after I arrived home, I received the call that she had passed away.

I followed Mother's wishes and had her body cremated. When my sister and her husband could travel again, we went to Florida and scattered her ashes at sea. The dolphins escorted us. Mom would have smiled.

John and I finally sold the historic powerhouse in November, just before the new house in town was completed. We had lived in that building longer than anywhere else in our lives. We'd spent a lot of time, money, and energy on that property. Our goodbyes were full of both gratitude and sorrow.

Our new home required very little interior maintenance, and the homeowners' association fees included professional groundskeeping. That made life easier and preserved his physical energy.

Those services also preserved my emotional energy. It was getting all the workouts it could handle. I stayed busy solving problems. I had the house paperwork to clean up, my mother's estate to settle, and day-to-day household matters to manage. I spent time with a few friends who provided opportunities to escape the stressful responsibilities and enjoy more ordinary activities and conversations.

More than two years after the initial diagnosis, the cancer treatments began to fail. Those last eight months were exceedingly emotional. We each had our own changes to face, and then, unbelievably, four months after John's decline became more significant, his mother passed away. He was a strong presence for his two younger sisters as the siblings grieved together during her last few days. He remained strong during the necessary cleaning, sorting, and organizing that needed to be done in her home. However, I could see the physical toll it took on him.

Death was a huge presence that week. All four of us focused on what needed to be done and avoided any recognition that we'd be doing this again in a different way. That was not a conversation we could manage. We had experienced enough loss. In eighteen months, our much-loved historic powerhouse and both of our mothers had been removed from our lives.

John was growing weaker in movement and energy, but his mind remained strong. We both knew our time together was approaching an end, yet we seldom talked about it. We talked about practicalities, but as usual, our discussions did not acknowledge our feelings. John was very introverted and private. Even after forty-seven years of marriage, he wasn't sharing his feelings. Neither was I. It's strange how I had learned to mirror his behavior.

After managing all the changes in my life and repeatedly putting pieces of my life together in new ways to fit new situations, I was working through just another new change. I waded through the treatments, the hope, his exhibited strength, and his decline. I went through a repeating mixture of avoidance, sorrow, sympathy, and anger. I began to accept that the inevitable was on its way. Subconsciously, and then consciously, I started waiting for the other shoe to drop. I was losing my husband. There was nothing I could do about it. Therefore, I focused on what I could manage—planning for my future.

Choreography and Caregiving

My life seemed like it was being choreographed or stage-managed. I would describe it to others at the time as "the music in my life keeps changing, but the dancing continues with new musicians, new rhythms, new costumes, and new sounds." There was a spiritual aspect to losing John. The angel and serendipity that had been with me all my life seemed to have joined together as a "Great Choreographer." They began supplying my life with new resources as each source of strength began to diminish.

Our friends, family, and people who were only good acquaintances became more supportive. They provided prepared food, shared trips, and hosted little celebrations. The meals, flowers, and even banana splits that would show up at our door at unexpected times were both amazing and surprising. And very welcome! They were a major blessing for our spirits and my energy.

People from my distant past contacted me out of the blue during John's last two weeks and sent sleep aids and books. The book *HELP, THANKS, WOW* by Anne Lamott was insightful, helpful, and thought-provoking. It focused on mindfulness of the three title words rather than grieving, but the change it created in my thinking was calming.

John's oldest friend and fraternity brother visited in early August. The two of them spent time talking about old times and life. I think, in many ways, Doug reassured John that he had accomplished what he needed to. The day after Doug left, John started letting go.

The next two weeks were very difficult. John, always the man in control, was managing his own medications. He kept a small book beside his chair in which he'd record each medication, time, and dosage. He was living in that chair, a big, man-size leather recliner in his office. He sat in it, worked in it, and slept in it.

Eight days before he died, John had a call with the man who would take his job. He asked me to stay in the room during his call and said, "If I start to sound crazy or say something stupid, just tell Allan I'm not myself anymore and hang up." They discussed contracts and contractors. John gave instructions on projects still to be finished. He gave cautions and advice on who to trust and who to watch. I'm sure Allan had heard that advice before, but John was delivering his final mentoring. Listening was tough to experience but filled me with pride. John's willpower and strength were so amazing. But they didn't last forever.

The next day, I noticed that he had missed one of his medications during the night. That afternoon, he was sleeping through another. I had to tell my husband that he was no longer capable of caring for himself. He had to release the last bit of independence and dignity.

I needed to feed him, literally spooning whatever food he could tolerate into his mouth. I had to help him use the bathroom. I had to measure all his medicines and be sure to give them at the appropriate time. As his pain increased, the hospice hotline gave me instructions for new dosages to administer in measurements that were different from the marking on the syringes and vials I had. Translating from ml to cc was a huge challenge for me. Nobody had bothered to tell me they were the same.

I needed something more secure and safe as he weakened. His leather recliner was no longer viable. I ordered a hospital bed for his office.

Keeping up with the dosing at the appropriate times was cutting into my sleep. Then, John started to try climbing out of bed on his own whenever he felt the need to use the bathroom. He was unaware that he couldn't support himself. I couldn't stay awake all night to monitor that, so I started interviewing home healthcare companies. Since I was uncomfortable with total strangers in my home while I was sleeping, I had a locksmith put a keyed lock on my bedroom door to let me sleep with confidence.

One morning, when I woke up, I found the night's caregiver asleep on the sunroom couch! That killed my confidence about leaving my husband in someone else's care. That was the end of my trying to care for him at home.

I had to move John to a hospice house that day and widowhood came much closer. For the well-being of both of us, keeping him in our home was no longer feasible.

The bittersweet week in the hospice home began with days full of his sleep and wakefulness. Although help and resources continued to be supplied, it was very difficult to share the experience of the life of a loved one coming to an end. The hospice caregivers were exceptional, caring primarily for John while also being supportive of my well-being.

My caregiving responsibilities were over. John was in good hands. I was relieved of the stress I had in caring for him at home. I no longer had to worry if I was doing enough or the right thing. I no longer feared I might be incorrectly administering the ml or cc doses of medicines. The stress of his illness wasn't over, but my worries about being inadequate diminished. I could breathe a little easier.

I sat near John's bed going through photos. I shared the captured stories with him that each photo generated. I talked to him about photos of family Christmases, crazy moments with his sisters, ski trips in Norway, explorations of Switzerland, college days and college friends, sailing adventures, anniversary trips, and the fourteen homes we'd shared. Sometimes he responded with a smile or a soft word. Each photo represented some part of the fifty-two years we'd had together; our forty-seven years of marriage and four years of college life. It was cathartic for me, and perhaps for him.

Each time there had been a change in our lives, John would say, "The adventure continues." So, there I sat, recounting our adventures. Until I couldn't sit there anymore. He began desperately struggling for breath. I couldn't stand there beside his bed. I couldn't stay in the room.

I'm ashamed that I was not at the bedside of my mother or husband in their final hour. The pain etched on my mother's face and the agony of my husband struggling to breathe were both more than I could endure. I left the room to avoid my pain. I couldn't watch the worsening deterioration. I didn't want to take that memory into my future.

I bailed out and left my loved ones in the company of a nurse they barely knew. Someone who would know just what to administer to ease their deaths. Someone who knew how to handle the end of life. But they weren't with someone they loved. I wasn't with them.

They were both heavily drugged for the pain. Would my being there with them have made a difference? I will never know. All I know is that I still am ashamed of leaving, even though I realize that at the time, my leaving was an act of self-preservation.

Since then, I've been told the romantic notion of being at the bedside of someone who is dying is often unrealistic. An easy slipping away into death is not always the case. Death can be ugly. Watching a loved one suffer when there is absolutely nothing you can do to change the inevitable is not a desirable final memory. It helped me to hear that.

As it turned out, avoiding the "ugly" part of death was unavoidable. I was required by state law to view his body in the casket and verify it was him. Shit!

Seeing my depleted husband in a formal military uniform that he had worn as a rigorous, younger man was devastating. So much for good final memories!! Damn laws!

The Realization of Transformation

Becoming a widow is a traumatic experience, but having the rug pulled out from under me was *not* a new experience. Having lived through my early and frequent lifetime changes and losses gave me the skills to manage my response to and recovery from the loss of my spouse.

Transitioning from being a wife to being a widow occurred in stages. I began to "transition" when I came to grips with the fact that my husband was terminally ill. After he died, we had a memorial service, but his burial would be delayed for an unknown amount of time. I had to wait for Arlington National Cemetery to tell me when the burial fit their schedule. In the meantime, I had many decisions to make, and tasks to manage. *Effective* and *efficient* are keywords in my vocabulary. So, that's what I focused on—the practical details that needed to be done.

The week between his death and the memorial service, I contacted MOAA. As John had said, they took care of the military survivor benefits pay issue for me. The funeral home had contacted Social Security, so I knew the survivor pay from that would eventually get solved and settled.

I notified the banks and changed the signature cards.

I called our investment advisor and told him of John's death. He gave me an amazing gift of a suggestion: "Karen, I will need to take John's name off all the joint accounts, and you may not be able to access them for a while. You may need money in the next few weeks or so. Why don't you take out $5,000 or $10,000? If you reinvest it in sixty days, there will be no penalty or tax implications." Although he was younger than me and his advice and suggestions were professional, I truly felt they were fatherly. As I hung up, I grinned to myself and said, "Thanks, Dad."

I canceled John's cell phone—or tried to. Having forgotten to record his password for the phone caused me all sorts of problems. The company wanted to text me with a code to verify I was an authorized user to close the account. Without his password, I couldn't receive the code. *That* challenge was a huge headache and took me months to resolve. Finally, after multiple communications and submitting the death certificate, I was able to close the account. Or, so I thought. I missed that he had a second device on the account, and Verizon didn't close that. Those bills arrived from the same provider as *my* cell phone and it took me four months to recognize the double billing and get that portion of his account closed. I was finally refunded six months after his death for a cell phone account that could have been closed in one week. Passwords—a blessing and a curse.

As John had declined, I realized that the home we bought for my widowhood was too big for just me. The expense of the mortgage would limit my financial flexibility. The "shutters and gutters" would consume my time and more of my money.

My passion was travel. I wanted to go and go now. A world was waiting for me with new sights to see, new people to meet, and new adventures to experience. I didn't want limits on my travel money.

While I wanted the ease and lower cost of living in a condo, I loved my new neighborhood. To give me an idea of what was in the area, my friend and realtor, Audrey, had shown me some condos earlier in the summer. I fell in love with one of them; however, I was in no position to make any changes at that time.

Two days after John's memorial service, Audrey called. The condo I loved was going back on the market the next week. Nine days after Audrey's call, and less than three weeks after John's death, I made an offer to buy it. After a bit of negotiating and bargaining, my offer was accepted. I was going to own a condo.

Talk about a change. Widowhood, divesting belongings, purchasing a home on my own, and moving all arrived at once. I had to rapidly and frantically reorganize my life. Good grief!

Maybe it actually was good for my grief. The hectic schedule that followed gave me very little time to grieve. My Great Choreographer began producing *The Life and Times of the Widow Karen*.

Perhaps the frantic schedule was a shield I erected. Yes, I had prepared myself emotionally for this eventuality, but I didn't take time to think about grieving over it. Not then.

As another gift from my Great Choreographer, I learned that the biannual community yard sale was scheduled for the weekend after I made an offer on the condo. Moving from 3,800 to 1,900 square feet required a lot of "weeding." I spent a frenzied week evaluating both what I wanted and what I needed in my new home. Everything else had to go, one way or another.

My yard sale was successful. I gave some of John's possessions to family members and friends so they would have a tangible memory of him. I sold a broad variety of things on Facebook Marketplace with surprising success. All the leftovers went to charity organizations.

In addition to disposing of furniture and personal items, I had to "dispose" of the house, as well. Audrey listed the house and, with my very reluctant agreement, held an open house three days later. The day after the open house, I had an offer. Audrey had been right. Ten days later, while I was at the title company signing papers to purchase my condo, the buyers for our house accepted my counteroffer. Great Choreography.

So it was that six weeks after John's memorial service, I had purchased a condo and accepted a purchase offer on our house. That weekend I collapsed. Nearly literally. I was severely dehydrated, dizzy, weak, and listless. I was scheduled to leave the next day for a grief recovery trip with friends. Instead, I spent the weekend on the couch with my water bottle, barely able to move to the kitchen.

When I did make those physically difficult forays to the kitchen, I had easy heat-and-serve meals. My freezer was full of many options from food that my friends had filled our home with over the summer. Not only was it restorative to my well-being, but consuming the foods accomplished the necessary pre-move freezer emptying.

After another two weeks of cleaning out, I began packing. Memories lived in the artwork and some of the furniture we had accumulated. My mother's and grandmother's crystal had to come with me, as did the handmade crocheted tablecloths I seldom use. Memories are important, but clutter is annoying. The decisions were difficult.

I packed about 150 boxes of various sizes and shapes. I didn't bother with boxes for the very breakable treasures; I left them out for the movers to pack. Precious and delicate items are insured against damage when the moving company packs them.

In all those previous moves, I learned that it is critical to account for every item loaded onto the moving van and to check that every item loaded is also unloaded into your new home. This requires multiple family members or friends because it can be very chaotic. Old friends who had also moved frequently knew the system and were an invaluable help to me.

Nancy helped me ensure all boxes were numbered. Dick watched them get loaded onto the truck. A few hours later, Dick checked the numbers off the inventory sheets as the boxes were delivered to the condo building. Nancy and I told the movers where to put each item in my condo.

Not surprisingly, we were exhausted at the end of the day. We went out to dinner, came home, made the beds, and collapsed into sleep. They left the next morning. So did I.

I had a car full of family furniture, linens, and other items that needed to be moved out of my car but not into my condo. They were destined for my sister Cindy, who now lived in Tennessee.

My dear friend Tammy drove down with me to unload my car and for an overdue visit with my sister. I had only seen her once since we scattered our mother's ashes eighteen months earlier. Life had been exceedingly busy for both of us.

The visit was short. I had hurt my knee during the hectic preparation to move. Wearing my Mighty Mouse persona, I thought I could lift anything and repeatedly carry heavy loads up flights of stairs. After all that lifting and toting and the long drive, my knee hurt badly. Plus, as much as I loved seeing Cindy, I had very little energy left for being a pleasant guest. I later learned I had pulled tendons and torn a meniscus. No wonder I wasn't in my best mood.

Tammy and I drove home two days after arriving at Cindy's. When I returned to my new condo, piles of boxes greeted me at the door. They were an overwhelming sight. Tammy helped me get the essentials out of the key boxes, but she had family events to attend.

There were no prepared meals in the house, but there must have been some food in the refrigerator. I think I ate something that night, but I was at the end of my rope. Two months and two weeks had passed since my husband's death. I wasn't done with this transition, but my body was stopping, much like it had after signing for my condo and accepting the buyers' agreement. I can only push myself so far out of necessity before reality steps forward and makes me stop.

However, magic happened the next day. In truth, I think Tammy instigated some behind-the-scenes manipulating that other caring friends fulfilled. My friend Margaret called and said, "Hey, Sweetie, Donna and I are going to be in your neck of the woods this week, so we're coming up to help you unpack."

Margaret lived in California and was going to be working in North Carolina. I lived in Maryland. That's not exactly close by. Donna lives in Los Angeles, and she was not coming east for work. Donna is Margaret's sister-in-law and one of the co-travelers on the 2014 trip to Morocco. She flew out for the sole purpose of helping me. She stayed for four days. Margaret flew in and out in two days. Together, those whirlwinds helped me unpack all my boxes and put nearly everything away. As we worked, the boxes were disassembled and hauled to recycling. During Donna's extended stay, she helped me hang most of the artwork in the house.

I was settled in. I could breathe again. My shoulders could relax. I could sit down.

My condo is the thirtieth home I have lived in. Moving wasn't usually this hard. But, other than my car full of belongings going to and from Florida for that first job, this was the first time I had moved alone. I couldn't have made the transition without all those friends.

When I look back now, the physical transition of moving into my condo was also a mental transformation. I was by myself. I was in a new home with furnishings and décor that I alone decided to keep and where to put.

Farewell to Part of My Life

I had spent four and a half months living in a small bubble of close friends and family. However, in January I had to face a much larger and distant collection of family and friends by myself. This time "by myself" made my self-assurance waver a bit.

Having served thirty-one years in the Army, John was eligible to be buried in Arlington National Cemetery. One disadvantage of that privilege, however, is that individual burials can be delayed for months as the cemetery staff arranges rites for multiple eligible soldiers.

John's funeral was scheduled for the middle of January, exactly five months after his death. By the time the ceremony occurred, I'd had time to recover from my marathon move, to adjust somewhat to a solo life, and to settle my emotions. Or so I thought.

I had chosen to give the eulogy for John, and I needed to get through without breaking. To avoid the triggers of shared emotions and maintain my composure, I distanced myself from friends and all except immediate family before the ceremony. Our small group waited in a side chapel until the chaplain escorted us into the sanctuary.

Just after I sat down, I heard soldiers enter the door at the back of the building. Emphatically clicking their metal-clad heels together, six uniformed soldiers started down the aisle carrying the flag-draped casket. As we all stood, the magnificent sound of the Army band crashed into the chapel from outside in thundering waves of horns and drums and the ethereal sound of flutes. I nearly lost that hard-won composure.

I had chosen hymns for the service, but I had envisioned them being played by the organist in the chapel. I hadn't realized the power of an Army marching band would be part of the ceremony. The grandiose sound of seventy musicians reached all the way down to my soul.

The casket I hadn't seen in five months was placed near the altar with pomp and ceremony. I clung to my husband's cousin beside me. I used every bit of self-control I had to keep from sobbing. I was overwhelmed. Military pageantry has always touched me. This was the final ceremony.

For the last three and a half years I had been saying to myself, "I can do this. I'm an Army wife." I repeated it as I stepped forward to deliver the eulogy. I repeated it again as I tentatively stepped back down the stairs, nearly losing my balance. I reached out to touch John's casket for balance, then smiled to myself as I realized I had needed his support to steady me one more time.

After the chapel service, John's casket was loaded onto a caisson drawn by six white horses. Behind it stood a soldier holding the reins of a riderless, yet saddled horse. As is tradition, a pair of backward-facing, black riding boots were in the stirrups.

As the band marched forward, playing "God of Our Fathers," a flag-bearing color guard and ten rows of soldiers followed. When they had all passed through the cemetery gates, the horses began carrying the casket to the gravesite. A line of cars full of civilians followed.

The casket was placed at the grave with military precision. The riflemen gave their gun salute. A distant solo bugler played Taps, the haunting twenty-four notes that signal the end of a military day. The flag was taken from his coffin, ritualistically folded, and then presented to me. It was over. A ceremonious farewell to being an Army wife.

Transition Realization

New experiences create new memories. I believe that continuing to create new memories is an essential part of healing after loss.

Our wedding anniversary was less than a week after the funeral. John and I had always taken a trip during the week around our anniversary. I decided that being away, as we always had been, was much more desirable than staying home and being gloomy or depressed. Heading for a faraway place seemed even more desirable, especially when a long-ago friend offered to join me.

I met my graduate school friend, Isabelle, in Madeira. She cared for me, pampered me with Portuguese pastéis de nata, listened to me, and helped chase away my sorrow. From champagne on a rooftop in our winter coats to cable car rides and garden tours, Isabelle arranged a week for recovery.

When I returned from Madeira, time slowed down. I had bought and sold homes, celebrated the holidays, buried my husband, and done some major traveling. The various responsibilities, opportunities, and distractions had kept me moving. Now, I was at home alone in the middle of winter. It was "downtime" in multiple ways. I had time to think about my loss, my changes, my feelings, my opportunities, and my choices.

There were days when guilt and sadness made me crawl into a shell. Staying in that shell was comfortable in a way. I could hide away from other feelings, other people, and other choices. It's a *lot* harder to be willing to crawl out of that shell than it is to crawl into it.

Thinking about that made me wonder how hermit crabs manage to settle into and move out of their shells. So, I opened Google. I learned that when a young hermit crab grows too big for her shell, she has to change. However, when she's fully grown, a hermit crab is just like me. Staying in or moving out of a shell is a matter of attitude.

A hermit crab always needs a shell to protect her soft underbelly. She especially needs it when she's molting and *all* of her body is vulnerable. Perhaps that's my explanation. I was molting, transitioning from a period of grief and waiting for my body to harden again.

Of course, I can't imagine a hermit crab ever feels guilty for staying deep in her shell. Perhaps, I didn't need to either.

The crab *does* need to eat, so she eventually emerges. I got hungry, too, and slowly emerged. My hunger wasn't for food, however. What got me moving was my appetite for time with my friends, travel plans, and productivity. But, yes, maybe some decent food, too.

Like the hermit crab, I had physically transitioned to a new home. My legal status transitioned from "married" to "widow." My *life* transitioned from wife to widow. I transitioned to being the sole decision-maker.

I had learned that I could live through loss, unhappiness, and disruption. I knew that managing any change takes finding opportunities, making good choices, and planning well.

I had a future to create.

Creating a Future

My social time didn't need as much "creation" as my private time. I had sufficient social interactions to meet my needs. My challenge was learning how to manage minute-by-minute aloneness.

There was a different tempo, soundtrack, rhythm, and staging to my days. That infernal TV or radio had always been on. Now there was silence. The everyday routines were not the same. The household chores were different. Mealtimes were strange.

No longer was there the responsibility of having dinner ready at 6:00. It no longer mattered when I cooked, or if I cooked at all. A handful of almonds or salmon and a salad sufficed. Vegetable soup and a salad for breakfast? Who's to judge whether my choices are appropriate or not? Really? Who would ever know?

If I had not prepared a meal at home in the past, John and I would go out to eat together. That option was gone. Now, I had to either call a friend or go alone. Dining out by myself was uncomfortable. I had to develop a comfort level, or at least identify the characteristics of when and where I could be comfortable dining out alone.

As a wife, I had always had the possibility of side conversations while reading the news or a book. Breaks had been filled with common activity rather than constant solo endeavors. I missed the silly yet easy option of finding my husband somewhere in the house and annoying him whenever I was bored or wanted to avoid the next thing on my to-do list.

Many individuals thrive on having time to be alone. I treasure time alone, too. However, for me, being with others is as essential as breathing.

Interacting with other people recharges my energy stores. Plus, humans are social creatures.

I've become more familiar and comfortable with aloneness. I still haven't established healthy eating practices and patterns, but I'm getting better. I have learned to live alone comfortably and contentedly. What a change.

Being alone also meant that I had to solve all my own problems. However, instead of compromising on the choices, I could choose the solution *I* wanted. I just had to remember that with all freedoms come responsibilities.

I love some of the choices I get to make, like choosing to have only pie for dinner, playing the music I love, or deciding what color to paint the master bedroom. Some of them are not much fun, like deciding whether to repair or replace the car, buy a service contract, get the air ducts cleaned, or trust a new service provider.

A new role and a new identity were forming. A new pattern for my life needed to be designed. Freedom to decide what to do, where, and when based only on what I wanted? Wow!

Making My Own Changes

In addition to my rapid move, I made other changes in my life after John died. I became involved with Woman to Woman Mentoring again. It had grown exponentially under the guidance of successive leaders. As a board member, I'm now one of those leaders. I have also mentored three young women and become friends with two of them.

I volunteered for one thing and then two for my condo association. I also briefly fulfilled an unexpired term on the condo board. I had bitten off more than I wanted to chew. A discussion with Rebecca and Tall Karen during one of our getaways gave me the oomph to tell the board president that I was going to step out of that major responsibility when the term was over. Ah, the value of friends.

I was active in my church as a teenager. Then we moved away, I started college, and I quit attending church. John and I fit the pattern of so many people. We only attended church on holidays. Several years after he died, I found a church and congregation that fit my needs and beliefs and became a member. I cannot say it was part of my healing process, but it has been part of my transformation.

I'm not writing about a faith journey here, so let me merely say that I like collectively celebrating my faith. I like the feeling of returning to something familiar, of having a common reason to gather, and the feelings of belonging and purpose. There was a self-confidence aspect, too. I entered that place and that relationship as an individual, not as part of a couple, and I was accepted as just me. As a widow, that was important to me.

Venturing Alone

Perhaps, it was all those weekend wanderings and frequent moves with my family. Maybe it was all the places I traveled with my husband during our thirty-one years of Army life. Whichever of them infected me with a travel bug, travel had become my passion. The most remarkable part of my transition has been traveling alone.

When John died, my friend Margaret suggested I use his American Airlines points for a trip before they expired. I spent those points on a ticket to the farthest place they would take me: Australia. The Great Choreographer stepped in to help again. I got the one remaining spot on a small educational tour with G Adventures.

In early March 2018, I stepped out of my comfort zone and took off for Australia. After nearly six hours of flying across America, I got on a fourteen-hour trans-oceanic flight. I was nearly seventy-one and by myself. It felt strange and a bit scary to head to the other side of the globe, knowing there was no one back home I could comfortably call to rescue me. No one would be diligently aware of where I was and what to expect. This new reality didn't stop me, but it most certainly gave me pause.

In our group of twelve travelers, five others were women of differing ages traveling alone. Strangely, I was disappointed that I wasn't the only adventurous female in the group. The surprising self-realization also created the hope of meeting other solo women travelers on the rest of my adventures. And I have.

A month after Australia, I went to the Azores and then to Morocco in May. I had fallen in love with Morocco on a trip with friends in the spring of 2014. The return trip was for two reasons. First, I wanted to research some details and places for a group trip I planned to host the next year. Second, to see my friend Jamal. Together we explored some new places I wanted to incorporate in the tour. I then discussed the possibilities with his boss and created the itinerary.

In 2019, I hosted that trip to Morocco. Rebecca, Tall Karen, and her husband, plus a handful of cousins, went with me. That's when we had the "revealing" Moroccan spa experience we mentioned in our introduction. After putting everyone on their return flights, I flew to Lisbon and extended my trip.

Taking off alone on a flight to a foreign country was no longer a new experience, nor was arriving alone. However, this time, not even a group of strangers were expecting me to join them. I was totally on my own. One week before my seventy-second birthday, I was a genuine independent traveler.

All of the travel and the various friends and experiences gave me time to discover the new me. I was becoming independent, braver, and more confident. I was also developing new interests and learning a lot.

It's a big world. I want to see as much as I can. My motto is: "All I can while I can." One of my sisters-in-law told me she was worried about me. She thought perhaps I was trying to escape or avoid reality and grief. I felt like I was becoming "free." I imagine others perceived my actions and behaviors with their own opinions, but everyone experiences widowhood differently. I wasn't escaping grief. I was discovering new and different things.

When we returned to the United States, John had been content with fewer trips and less adventurous ones. I thrive on exploring the new and different. I had been chomping at the bit to get away from everyday life. Anyone who had known me for my entire life wouldn't have been surprised. I've always gone full steam ahead on most things. It's just my style.

All I Can While I Can

That motto becomes more meaningful during stressful times in my life. I was hobbled by knee surgery in the summer of 2019. To make up for lost time, I planned and registered for a lot of really great trips for 2020.

I managed to spend New Year's Eve week in Buenos Aires and eleven days on a trip to Antarctica in January. As I had hoped on my first solo trip to Australia, I made a friend on that trip. She was my cabin mate on the boat to Antarctica.

I visited with friends in Puerto Vallarta and then spent nearly a week with my father. In early March 2020, I enjoyed a long weekend in New Orleans and returned home as the world was changing.

My "All I can while I can" travel came to a halt. A global pandemic smashed my plans for a two-week trans-Atlantic sailing trip, a two-week trip to Alaska, twenty days in Mongolia, and a short hop to Bermuda. The whole world came to a stop with COVID-19.

While others spent much of the quarantine deep-cleaning their homes, I used my time to plan another group trip for 2021. We were going to explore Armenia, Georgia, and elements of the Silk Road. That didn't happen either.

I also spent time writing. I wrote that book people often say they are going to write someday. Perhaps it was not having someone at home to converse with. Perhaps, it was the feeling that I had wisdom to share and no children to whom I could pass it down. It could have been the world change we were all experiencing. Maybe I missed teaching, facilitating, and working with others on ideas. Whatever the impetus, I wrote a memoir that recounted my life full of changes. The title was *Here We Go Again!*.

I gave copies to my nieces and grandniece and donated copies to a few cohorts of mentees. Many of my friends and family read it, along with a few others. I sold about fifty copies and then took the book off the market. It served its purpose as a memoir for my family. As I look back, I now see that it was also my "healing book." As I was finishing the book, I had more healing to do, but maybe the writing helped.

Death and Grief on Repeat

As part of all that reminiscing, I called my sister on Easter morning in 2020. I wanted to tell her I'd been thinking about something her grandson had done one long-ago Easter morning. Cindy had not been in the best of health for the past few months, and I wanted to cheer her up with some good memories and laughs. We had a great conversation. Three days later, her husband took her to the hospital.

Nine days later, I was lying in bed saying my prayers when I could sense Cindy next to me. I reached out and could feel myself holding her hand. We had a mental conversation about our lives and experiences as I alternately laughed, wept, and sobbed. Then, she was gone as ethereally as she had arrived.

At three o'clock the next day, Cindy's husband called me to tell me she had been put on a respirator the night before. Before suppertime, Cindy was gone. My little sister, who had been the only constant friend in my child-hood and the detail-oriented sounding board of my adulthood, was gone.

My life changed. I can't say it changed the way I spend my days or any framework by which we measure time, attitude, or health. The fabric of my life just has another hole in it.

My concept is that as each loved one dies and leaves another hole in our hearts, we place a basket in that hole in which we store the memories, images, emotions, magic, and love we shared with that loved one. Sometimes, the baskets topple over or need repair. That's why we have friends. They help us clean up the mess, pick up the pieces, undo the corners, tape up the tears, and refill the basket.

Cindy's death was a huge unexpected change that pulled the rug out from under me in ways my husband's death hadn't. Her death drastically affected our father.

Although initially a pleasant situation, my father's living in a continuing care community was a drastic inconvenience during COVID-19. The pandemic's rapid growth had closed nearly every eldercare facility in the country.

Dad lived in Michigan on lockdown. I lived eight hours away in Maryland. He lived on the second floor, so I couldn't even visit him through a window. I had to tell my father over the telephone that his youngest daughter had died.

Over the next few months, he wouldn't answer his telephone or emails. I worked with the staff to help me get him on the phone and ensure he had extra attention and support, but he became ill.

My friend Tall Karen had offered to drive me up to clean out his apartment before his illness became quite severe. But then I was told he was failing fast. Since I was still not allowed to enter the facility for a visit, Karen and I chose to wait a bit. We planned to leave when I was told the end of Dad's life was approaching.

We left thirty minutes after I got the call. Eight hours later, we were only twenty minutes away from his facility when he died. It was less than four months after my sister had passed. I now had no immediate family members still alive.

I never got to exchange a last word. I could not be present for the final days or the death of my last two nuclear family members because of COVID restrictions. I cannot fully imagine the emotions of a woman who was unable to be with her husband as he died because of the same restrictions.

Karen and I cleaned out Dad's apartment while I also notified the family and arranged a gravesite service. The same COVID requirements nullified a funeral.

Our drive from Michigan back to Maryland was a long one. Tall Karen and I had lengthy conversations about the practical responsibilities I still had to manage and about the emotions of losing a father and a husband. Then the conversations turned to Rebecca. Her husband had died five months earlier.

Karen and I needed to be respectful of Rebecca's feelings and her experience with grief. But, we had been down similar paths and wanted to support her in whatever ways we could. Although we couldn't visit her in person, we created a plan for collective communications to check on her frequently, engage her in ideas, and support her. We created a group on Messenger with a fun name referring to our experience in Morocco.

Orphaned Elder

I previously talked about holes in our hearts, but I sometimes feel like I live in a donut's hole. I've lost all my nuclear family. No parents, no siblings, no spouse. Never any children. I'm all alone with a ring of friends, acquaintances, and supporters around me who are near and dear. However, I'm still all alone in that hole. I'm not moaning. I'm blessed with that donut around me. Sometimes, I just really miss the filling.

Becoming what has been called an "orphaned elder" or "elder orphan" has been one of my more difficult adaptations. We orphaned elders are people who have crossed into our seventies and beyond and no longer have family or significant others. Although there are friends and neighbors, what will happen when dementia or disabilities set in? Who will even initially identify the problems? In a discussion during a session with my longtime massage therapist and friend, she told me she'll let me know when my brain is no longer functioning well. But, then there will be caregiving issues. Who will manage those details? The possibility of both physical and financial abuse and manipulation will exist. I've heard stories of physicians ignoring the expressed wishes of a patient recorded in a legal, medical directive. It's a very uncomfortable position to be in. I don't have all the answers yet.

I've taken steps to minimize some of the challenges. I've known the children of some friends all of their lives. Should I become disabled temporarily or permanently, one of those daughters has agreed to manage my money. There will still be accounts to manage, bills to pay, and financial business to conduct as long as I'm alive. I know she has the professional skills to make the task less difficult than it might be for others. Plus, I can personally trust her.

The daughter of another friend is a lawyer. She will manage the innumerable details of closing my estate when I die. I remember how much work it was for me to do both of these things for my parents, and I will be eternally grateful to these younger women for agreeing to take on these responsibilities.

Celebrations

I turned seventy-five in 2022. After two-plus long years of pandemic restrictions and losing all my immediate family members, I decided it was a great time to celebrate life. I wanted to thank all the people who were still in my life and had added so much sparkle to my years. I gave myself a big party. Friends and family came from around the country and from my current hometown. After many decades of moving around, I had now lived in one place for more than two decades. That was another detail worth celebrating.

Karen, Rebecca, and I started celebrating our friendship and love of travel by doing small activities together and taking annual escapes in the middle of the winter. Remembering the wonderful, although embarrassing, experience we had in Morocco, we found a Moroccan spa about an hour from where Tall Karen and I live and another near Rebecca's new home in Ohio.

We had an amazing week exploring the area around Santa Fe. As we were heading home, we even discovered the balloon festival in Albuquerque.

After Santa Fe, our next long trip was to Sedona in 2023. It was magical from the first night. There is something mystical about those rocks beyond their beauty.

When I went to graduate school in Norway, I engaged with classmates from twenty-three different countries. I am still friends with many of them. Integration with people from other cultures provides knowledge, understanding, and respect, which I value. I wanted to encourage and enable more students to study in a foreign country for at least some of their post-secondary education. With a unique sense of celebration, I took some of the investments I received when my father died and established the Karen S. Justice Scholarship for Study Abroad Fund. There's a link to it on the Resources page if you want to learn more about it or know someone who may want to apply.

My Lessons on Feelings

My multiple moves throughout elementary school meant my arithmetic classes were always a bit disconnected. I now feel like I'm missing a few connections in the logic of numbers. The little gremlins in my head pop up now and then to say, "Oh, no. You can't do that. You've never been any good at that." They frightened me when I had to manage the doses of John's medicine. They made me uncomfortable as I bought my condo and sold our home.

I have worked with budgets and financial statements in my jobs, and although I labored over them at times, I was perfectly capable of doing the work. When I was trying to settle insurance policies, manage investment decisions, and create a new budget as a widow, those little gremlins were constantly whispering in my ears.

I reminded myself of once reading that our perceived weaknesses may simply be underdeveloped strengths. I may have been challenged by my early arithmetic classes but my skills with numbers were eventually "developed." That thought helps me ignore those nasty gremlins. I have conquered my past and can give myself permission to feel confident.

Sometimes I feel like I should have learned more or done more earlier in life. While at one of our writing get-togethers, I was whining about what I could have or should have done if only I'd made better choices or been smarter. Rebecca turned to me and said, "Your life tapestry doesn't include conquering the world at age seventy-six, Karen. Yes, you could have made those decisions, but you would not be where you are now. Don't dismiss what you did. Based on what you have experienced, you have learned the value of helping others."

It helps to have good friends. The near void of long-term friends I experienced earlier in my life has been replaced by circles of flourishing, invaluable friendships. The people I've worked with on various boards and committees, the new friends at church, and the very personal relationship of "Rebecca and the Two Karens" are friendships that have grown over the years.

A few women in my condo and I created a *tribe* during COVID-19, sequestering ourselves in shared spaces six feet apart. We've all developed closer relationships with each other that include some form of mutual dependency.

I now feel that desired sense of belonging.

A New Love

I've been widowed for more than seven years now. I miss John's thoughtful generosity. I miss his intelligent insights. I miss not having him in the next chair to discuss the morning news or what I had just seen out the window. I don't miss the frustration I had in trying to communicate with him at times. Our different personalities were often as challenging as they were enhancing. I don't miss the little squabbles. I don't miss regular dinner hours or the noisy TV shows he liked to watch. I miss his crazy sense of humor. He could write the loveliest of love notes. He filled my earlier life with laughter, joy, adventure, and love. I have a magnet on my refrigerator that says, "What is life but one grand adventure." Love is a grand adventure, too.

By the time this book is published, it will be ten years since I learned of John's fatal disease. That's a lot of time to work on a new personal, solo future. I'm happy with what I've developed. I'm also happy that my future is not totally "solo."

I was blessed with an amazing, magically successful Match.com experience. One of the most valuable riches of my new life is my new life partner.

Jeff enriches my life with intelligent conversations. He's a college business professor, and I love talking about business ideas with him. He challenges my strategic thinking in games of Scrabble, backgammon, rummy, and sometimes bridge.

Jeff's not in the next chair when I read the news, but he does reply to my cut-and-paste emails about some idea or comment I share. We cook together, and we love traveling together—when he's not teaching. He's a great listener and patient. He makes me laugh. I love how he holds me. He's shared his family and friends with me and vice versa. I'm blessed that they have accepted me as part of his life.

Jeff and I have no plans to marry or even live together. Jeff lives forty minutes away, which is less than great, but we each have a very fulfilling life in our individual communities. We fulfill each other's lives in ways beyond what we had previously experienced. We are partners for life.

He also writes beautiful, romantic love notes. I am blessed.

New Changes and New Chapters

Widows are faced with the necessity of starting a new life and creating a future that is different from what they had envisioned. Losing a spouse changes us, but it isn't the end of us.

What I was doing in the past differs from what I am doing now. I have new and different chapters in my life. However, I haven't lost the old me.

Like the ancient cities of the world, I've just continued to build on top of what was there before. The ruins of the Roman Forum look like they fell or dropped below the surrounding modern city when, in reality, the city was built on top of the ruins. Pieces were pulled from the ancient structures and used to build new ones.

Every widow has those opportunities, too. Like me, it's possible to build upon the foundations of the past and pull the significant pieces forward to build new structures. The building may take time, but the foundations remain as the new structures develop on top. I've been through a lot, but I've gained a lot, just like those old cities.

My transition and transformation have been multifaceted. They've included changes in housing, volunteering, travel, freedom, friendships and relationships, daily routines, diet, budget, attitudes and behaviors, and even clothing styles to some degree.

I have more time for those lingering weekday lunches and Happy Hours with friends that working women dream about. I relish having time to travel where and when I wish. I have new friends and new goals. I've learned new skills and initiated new opportunities for others. My connections to my community have increased. In addition to the richness and purpose I find in my volunteer responsibilities, writing my first two books and working with Rebecca and Karen on this book have added purpose.

Life may throw me into unexpected situations and, sometimes, knock me sideways, but I feel grounded and surrounded by a dependable network of people who act as my safety net. I truly love my life now as a retired widow. I am content and happy.

◘　◘　◘

Frank and Rebecca at their niece's wedding reception, 2012

Rebecca's Story

Unexpected News

Tuesday. Just like any other. Until it wasn't.

I sat on the stairs by the front door, waiting for Frank to come home from work. Earlier that day, I received a phone call while driving home from a meeting. The caller was the doctor who had done my biopsy to rule out endometrial cancer. At that time of the biopsy, he told me with the confidence physicians must learn in "Bedside Manner 101" that I "looked clean." "Looked clean" is the medical euphemism for "no cancer seen."

The doctor asked if I had time to talk. After telling him I was driving, he said, "You have endometrial cancer. Let's schedule a hysterectomy."

You fucking idiot. I just told you I was driving, and you dropped that bomb? roared through my brain. I told him I would seek a second opinion and hung up.

I was a registered nurse for thirty years. After thirty years of working in multiple levels of the healthcare system, I had the knowledge and clinical expertise to know what was coming. I know too much, and I expect too much. I have a love/hate relationship with the healthcare system.

And so, I sat on the stairs, waiting.

Frank finally came home and stopped on the landing, looking at me strangely. His routine lab results had come back. His PSA had increased from a standard range to a high number, indicating potential prostate cancer.

It was an ugly Tuesday.

Six weeks after being told I had endometrial cancer and Frank's news of prostate cancer, I had a hysterectomy. Fortunately, my lesion was minimal and had not penetrated the muscle or muscle wall of the uterus. I was declared cancer-free after the surgery.

Now is the time also to tell you I am neurodivergent—my brain works differently and is physically different. I have the ability to file information in the deep archives of my brain. The archives are like an infinite collection of books that have been read, closed, and stuck on a dusty shelf, rarely to be opened again. The library in my archives is vast. Rarely are my memories "pictures or movies." Instead, the memory appears as words, similar to chyrons on television news shows. I read my memories. And if I am not actively thinking and focusing on what my brain is doing, I hear my brain counting—*thirteen, fourteen, fifteen* . . . and onward. I am able to follow two different lines of thought simultaneously, which occasionally caused problems during my school years.

I have auditory sensory sensitivity, which means I am very sensitive to sound and have a low tolerance for loud noises as they cause me pain. Additionally, I experience a form of synesthesia, where I perceive loud noises as colors. The most painful noises appear as white explosions that fill the entirety of my internal vision. Other types of noise have their own colors.

I find peace in solitude. I cannot tolerate the energy of crowds. I am a recluse by nature and preference. I can force myself to participate in crowd activities such as conferences, but my attention, time, and energy are limited. I am selective in my friendships. If my brain or nervous system gets overwhelmed, my brain shuts down; I see only blackness. I can get lost in processing information in my brain and not see or hear things around me. I always thought this was a secret known only to me until the morning I took my older son and his fiancée to breakfast. In a far distant place in the back of my head, I heard her say to my son, "Your mom is staring at me." He replied, "No, she doesn't even see you. She's in her head."

First Marriage and the Army

I met my sons' father on the first day of nursing school. It was a fraught relationship from the beginning, but I held onto the naive and youthful romantic dream that we would live happily ever after and grow old together. Sixteen years later, I realized I was losing my sense of self at the deepest possible level. It was time for me to save my life. I filed for divorce. It would be six years before I would remarry.

While I struggled through "divorce feelings" I was utterly unfamiliar with, some powerful force kept calling me to obtain my doctoral degree. I joined the U.S. Army Reserve Nurse Corps because the Army would pay for my doctoral education. I was assigned to a Combat Support Hospital in Indianapolis. I held a position that was outside the norm for a nurse. I held the combined positions of S2 (personnel) and S3 (training, planning operations for deployment). My time in the Reserves coincided with the beginning of the first Gulf War, Operation Desert Storm.

Operation Desert Shield/Desert Storm

At the beginning of the war, my job was to help prepare the Army Reserve units from Indiana for deployment to the Persian Gulf. I had a great team who traveled with me throughout the state. We made sure everyone's paperwork was in order and completed. Of course, the paperwork included forms designating significant others in case of the soldier's death, a plan of care for surviving children and spouses, insurance forms, etc.

If I've ever had a single act in my military career that I am most proud of, it occurred during one of those deployment preparations. A young female soldier came to me on the verge of hysteria. I learned she had just returned from basic training two weeks earlier. Her husband—also a soldier—had been killed in a training accident. The Army released her to a reserve unit to finish her contract. She had an infant and no local relatives to care for the child if something happened to her. I collected the chaplain traveling on my team and went to her commanding officer. Even though I had no authority, I informed the officer I would not clear this woman for deployment to the Gulf and asked him to amend her orders for desk duty at her home station. He agreed.

I was put on active duty in my reserve unit during the war. My daily job involved going to the reserve station, where I fielded phone calls from parents and lawmakers. I helped families of deceased soldiers navigate the required paperwork. I disappointed mothers who wanted me to bring their sons home because "the fiancée might break up with him." Bringing soldiers home from a war zone was, as they say, "above my pay grade."

Just as I had prepared the soldiers for deployment, I was responsible for debriefing them upon their return. During interviews with members of my unit, I noticed a pattern of strange and unexpected health issues. It was later I suspected I had probably been one of the first to document symptoms of Gulf War Syndrome. Indeed, it was later determined that the first indicators of Gulf War syndrome were documented in Reserve Units from Indiana.

Being a nurse in my unit position allowed me to see health aberrations that an engineer or logistics specialist would not have noticed. I documented the issues, wrote a memorandum to my commanding officer documenting these health problems, and suggested they warranted further inquiry.

My meticulous work organizing files and preparing personnel earned my first entry into Army Nurse Corps history. I received the General Douglas MacArthur Leadership Award. I met Mrs. Jean MacArthur, who, at age ninety-seven, was still deeply in love with the man she called "my General."

I excelled at this Army life and transferred to active duty. Active duty was my escape from Indiana and the daily intrusions of my divorce. My first posting was at the United States Army Medical Research Institute for Infectious Diseases in Frederick, Maryland. I became the Clinical Research Protocol Nurse for all the clinical vaccine trials. My organizational skills and knowledge about conducting rigorous scientific trials were put to good use. Additionally, I was responsible for the health of the Medical Research Volunteers who participated in the trials.

Since soldiers in my position usually rotated for four years, I bought a house in a small rural town close to the Institute.

Distinguished Professor Alert

One day, as I walked down the hall of my division, I noticed a gentleman leaning against a counter. He didn't work at the Institute—I knew most employees. As I casually walked past him, my brain reported, *Distinguished Professor Alert.* I scanned for a wedding ring and saw none. I did have a bit of a mental hiccup when I observed his beat-up deck shoes.

The Distinguished Professor (Frank, a highly regarded scientist) became an institute employee. Science brought us together. Frank volunteered as a subject in a vaccine trial to meet me. Our brains attracted each other as magnets to iron. We were equivalent in that we lived in our brains. Quickly, we learned we were more compatible than just our magnetic brains. Frank was also solitary and more comfortable with a very small group. Given our propensity to be alone and away from too much energy and how we could get so lost in our brain work that we were unreachable, we learned we both were on the spectrum of neuro-divergence. To our surprise, when we told this to people who knew us, they responded, "Yeah, we knew."

With the active encouragement of people throughout the Institute, we eventually dated and married. I kept my maiden name since we were professionals with multiple scientific publications to our respective names. Plus, after my divorce, I felt strongly against taking on another man's name.

Who Was Frank?

Frank was of Czech-Slovak ancestry. His father was American Czech; his mother was American Slovak. He did not speak English until he started kindergarten at age seven. He recounted that he was furious with his parents for not teaching him English. He was so angry that when a teacher mispronounced his surname, he adopted that pronunciation to "get back" at them.

Frank was born nine months after the birth of his older brother. The brother became ill, and the family's pediatrician thought injecting antibiotics into the infant's spinal column seemed like a good idea. The doctor damaged a beautiful, bouncing baby so severely that the child had to be institutionalized. Frank's mother became profoundly depressed and could not bond with him as a newborn or throughout childhood. His brother died at age twelve while he was still institutionalized. The young Frank learned that healthcare providers were not to be trusted. He carried that fear to his death.

We were each other's "safe place" away from crowds, noise, and things that didn't interest us. Over the course of our twenty-five-year marriage, our favorite activity was browsing in secondhand book-stores. Frank amassed a personal library that filled two entire walls of bookshelves.

Once in a while, I would travel to professional meetings with Frank—and he became a different man! He was talkative, actively funny, and working the crowds. He was . . . an extrovert! Who was this man?

Traveling with Frank was an adventure in high anxiety. He hated to fly. If it were possible to drive to Europe from the U.S., he would have done so. If we traveled to the interior of some countries, he was terrified his seat partner would be a goat or a chicken. He had no confidence in an airline that provided passenger seats to animals. The greatest extreme that saved Frank from traveling to a foreign country was a civil war that erupted the day before we were to depart.

Working Through Our Stuff

Frank was also divorced, so we had a few things to work out. It took a few confrontations before we realized we were responding to past experiences with our exes and not each other. We developed a ritual line: "Just because 'this' happened in your first marriage doesn't mean that's what's happening now."

In our twenty-five and a half years together, we had only two major arguments. The first involved a mouse. My house (now our house) was in a rural area. As more cropland was converted to housing, the field mice migrated. Our cat alerted us to a mouse in the kitchen. We formed a tunnel with couch cushions through the kitchen and out the back door. The cat chased the mouse through the tunnel to the outdoors.

The mouse invasion continued. We set out traps. SNAP! I checked the trap and realized, with horror, that the mouse was still alive. We loudly argued about who was going to be merciful to the mouse. Neither of us wanted to be a mouse killer. Finally, Frank put the mouse out of its—and our—misery. The act was so unlike Frank's usual behavior that his face reflected a piece of his soul cracking.

Our second argument was protracted, and we couldn't identify precisely what was happening. About six months into the problem, I was in the shower and achieved "shower enlightenment." Our problem resulted from our beliefs about each other's capabilities. Frank was an incredibly intelligent man. His scientific accomplishments were known throughout the world. He was capable of producing new knowledge worth a Nobel Prize. He felt the same about my intelligence and capabilities. The "problem" was neither of us felt the other was achieving their maximum potential, and we were frustrated by that perceived lack of ambition. After presenting my shower enlightenment, we had an invigorating conversation and understood neither of us wanted to exert the energies required to achieve a Nobel or any other major prize.

Over the years, we collaborated on the occasional scientific paper. My statistics background was stronger than his, so he often asked me for understanding and advice about statistics. I created visual graphics for several of his papers. He always credited me.

Our everyday lives were a perfect yin-yang of skills and preferences. Frank loved working in the yard and took on all the yard-related activities. I do not enjoy outdoor activities but am very good with power tools and paintbrushes. I was the person who designed, built, rearranged, painted, and wallpapered anything inside the house. Anything beyond our capabilities, we hired out.

Kids

Between the two of us, we had four children: my two sons and his two daughters. My boys were considerably older than Frank's girls. I was in my early to mid-twenties when the boys were born. Frank hadn't married the first time until he was in his late thirties. His girls were small children when their parents divorced.

A memorable conversation occurred one time the girls were visiting. We were driving, and from the back seat, the question arose, "Dad, how come you're older than Becky, and her boys are older than us?" I immediately answered, "My boys are older because I married when I was twelve." Flabbergasted silence ensued.

Despite Frank being divorced for approximately six years before meeting me, the girls were angry and decidedly did not like me. I understood they felt protective of their mother, but their behaviors were often less than delightful. In their eyes, and through the impact of others' conversations, I was the evil stepmother because I "took" their dad and enforced standards and boundaries. I wasn't going to accept hateful and avoidant behaviors from them. Little did the other adults feeding their behaviors know that I encouraged their dad to strengthen his relationship with them because I cared about their well-being and their future relationships with men.

The girls have grown into successful, brave women with beautiful families. Now, we keep in touch with each other almost every week through texting and social media.

The Army No More

Our marriage stopped any further movement in my military career. Fort Detrick was the only place in the world where Frank could do his research. I was not willing to move anywhere else without him. As a "why not?" action, I applied for a Medical Research Fellowship at Walter Reed Army Medical Center. Historically, this fellowship was awarded only to Army physicians who wanted to conduct research. Two Army nurses were the first nurses ever selected for the fellowship; I was one of the two.

This was my second entry into Army Nurse Corps history.

The research I conducted during my fellowship was the basis for my doctoral thesis. I submitted my completed research to the annual research symposium for Army nurses. I was awarded the Phyllis J. Verhonick Nursing Research Award for Excellence in Nursing Research.

This was my third entry into Army Nurse Corps history.

I spent one more year at Walter Reed and found myself increasingly unhappy. Being in the Army no longer accurately described who I was. My daily drive to the hospital on one of the major thoroughfares to Washington, D.C. could range from one and a half to three hours, depending on traffic and/or accidents. The day I looked over at the driver in the next lane and saw him reading the *Washington Post* while driving seventy miles per hour was the day I decided to resign my commission.

When I left the Army, Frank supported every decision I made. He was also my greatest advocate. He may not have been my willing travel partner, but he wholeheartedly endorsed my travels.

"Frank, I'm going to India for a month to work with a physician in an ashram."

"Frank, I'm traveling to Myanmar for two weeks with a Japanese Buddhist monk."

The Buddhist monk had brought enough money to purchase seven tons of rice for a village. He did not bring the actual rice because it would have been confiscated. I was asked to present the money to the village elders, and I agreed. We hoped no one would want an international incident involving a white-haired American woman. (I do not recommend anyone else try this stupid bravado.) Thankfully, the transfer of money went well. I have the pictures to prove it.

When I began my photography/art career, Frank encouraged me every step of the way. He was the gentle driving force that led me to open a very successful studio on Main Street in our town. If we were at any art event where my artistic works were displayed, he became the extrovert and "Frank, my PR manager." He was so good at it that I asked him to become a business partner, but he was more comfortable praising my work publicly on a limited basis. Given we were both solitary people, I understood.

The Beginning of the End

Frank opted for radiation therapy for his prostate cancer. He refused any other types of treatment. His PSA levels did drop; there was no remission, but the levels headed in the right direction. Strangely, though, he started having trouble breathing on occasion. He had a story for every experience of breathlessness. The story he used most often was "The air is too cold and makes it hard to breathe."

My focus became fighting for precise information from his doctors, asking the questions Frank would not ask, and researching any treatment options presented. Soon enough, his PSA jumped back up to an even higher number, and indeed, his cancer was spreading throughout his abdomen. Of all the options offered, Frank chose hormone therapy. His physician told Frank he would have side effects one would see in menopause! Frank didn't know what that meant, nor did the doctor explain.

The shortness of breath became a constant, and he became weaker. He convinced himself he was experiencing "menopause." Having experienced menopause myself, I knew these were not menopausal symptoms. He refused to go to the doctor. He would hide his feelings or illnesses behind silence. He was very good at discussing politics with his physician rather than talking about his own health.

Then COVID-19 made itself known to the world.

One night in late March 2020, he told me he had not felt so bad since he had experienced food poisoning. His color was gray, and the man who had been a walking furnace was cold and clammy to the touch. I asked him to tell me what he *felt* in his body, not what he *thought* was happening.

I could not get a blood pressure reading or feel his pulse. Quickly, I realized he was having a heart attack. I told him he was having a heart attack and that we needed to get to the hospital. He refused because he was "afraid to catch COVID" in the hospital.

The next morning, a Friday, I almost had to drag a severely weakened Frank out of the house. He consented only to see his physician, so that's where we went. As he shuffled into the exam room, I told his doctor that Frank had signs of a heart attack and congestive heart failure. The physician ignored me and, without doing any kind of physical assessment, declared that Frank only needed an inhaler. At this blow-off, I demanded that Frank tell the doctor exactly what he had told me when describing how he felt. Suddenly, his physician thought doing an EKG might be a good idea. He was surprised to see that Frank was in atrial fibrillation with a heart rate of over 150 beats per minute. This meant Frank's heart was beating at a high rate that was rapidly becoming life-threatening.

At this point, the doctor suggested I drive Frank to the regional cardiac center ninety minutes away—on one of the busiest interstates in the country! When I stated Frank needed to be transported by ambulance, the doctor replied, "There's no traffic on the interstate because everyone's staying home because of COVID. You should get there in an hour."

Have I mentioned my love/hate relationship with the healthcare system?

I put Frank in a wheelchair, pushed him to the car, and started the drive. Frank kept nodding in and out of sleep—or was it unconsciousness? As I watched his head bob, my brain whirled through plans I might need. Plan A: Could I pull off to the side of the road, drag Frank from the car, and do CPR without both of us being flattened by an eighteen-wheeler? Plan B: Pray he wouldn't die while I was driving. I opted for Plan B and kept driving. I could feel my anger rising.

In my memory, everything was gray. The sky was gray. The lights were gray. Neighborhoods were gray. Frank was gray.

I registered him at the emergency room desk when we finally reached the hospital. I told the women behind the desk that he was having a heart attack and was in atrial fibrillation. Standard protocol is that people with signs/symptoms/complaints of heart attack are supposed to be seen immediately. I was told to wait to be called.

Ten minutes . . . *Those three people don't look in distress. WTF! Why are they taking up resources?*

Fifteen minutes . . . *Okay, that guy holding his hand up in the air, wrapped in a blood-dripping towel, should be seen now.*

Twenty minutes later, we still sat in the waiting room as Frank became more critical and closer to death. Just as I stood up to storm the desk and start screaming, Frank was called back into the ER. Suddenly, all the action was focused on Frank.

Have I mentioned my high expectations for our healthcare system? I'm frequently disappointed.

My angry determination pushed through Frank's reticence, gross medical mistakes, and generalized confusion about COVID-19; he was finally admitted to the regional heart hospital. Doctors told me Frank was less than three hours away from dying and had less than thirty percent heart function. A cardiac surgeon performed emergency surgery for stent placement. He was scheduled for bypass surgery the following day.

But I knew he was not a candidate for successful surgery; he was too ill, too weak, and too close to death when admitted. The bypass surgery was a gigantic Hail Mary attempt. Frank realized his only chance to live was to have the surgery, so he consented. I briefly debated telling him his odds and what he would experience but decided against it. He was already terrified, and he wanted to live. I knew the outcome but allowed myself to pretend he would survive the surgery.

We had a little ritual in which we would ask each other, "Have I told you lately that I love you?" Before he left for the operating room, I asked, "Have I told you lately that I love you?" He gave me his joking, quizzical face, suggesting he was trying to remember if I had. As he was rolled out the door, I said, "I love you."

I called his daughters and delivered the news. Both lived across the country from us. I told the girls not to come because the hospital would not permit their visit. In fewer than twenty-four hours, the policy to prohibit *any* visitors would go into effect. At that point, even I could not be with Frank. I wasn't allowed to sit in the hospital lobby because they didn't want people in the lobby to spread the COVID-19 virus. I had to make phone calls outside in the cold wind of a gray March. I made a reservation for a late arrival at a hotel about two miles from the hospital.

Post-Operative

Through force of habit, I scanned all the numbers and graphs on monitors and the respirator when I was finally allowed in the room at 11:30 p.m. He was surrounded by a metal forest of IV poles, along with the multiple bags of fluids and medications hanging like overripe fruit ready to drop. His endotracheal tube—one of the least comfortable pieces of equipment—hung from his mouth in the most undignified manner.

He's already dead. I saw it. His skin color was a waxy pale yellow, not the color you would expect to see with a newly perfused heart. I felt the absence of his consciousness. The staff was cheerful that he was doing well and would be extubated later that night. I was stunned. They could not see what I saw, what I knew.

I left for the hotel.

I reached the hotel shortly after 1:00 a.m., and I sat in bed with the TV on for background noise. I wasn't thinking, and I wasn't sweating with worry. I just sat there. I dozed off at about 2:00 a.m.

Eventually, they removed his endotracheal tube and, in fewer than thirty seconds, realized Frank was unresponsive. They proceeded with emergency life-saving measures, probably knowing their efforts would be in vain.

I received the call in my hotel room at 3:30 a.m. I drove to his hospital bedside.

The sad irony was that everything Frank did not want to happen to him did. Once he consented to the bypass surgery, the physicians and hospital had to assume intent to live, regardless. And that included reopening his chest in the ICU and performing manual cardiac massage.

Sometimes, I know too much.

I slumped into a chair at the foot of Frank's bed, speechless and hollow. The room was now empty of machines and poles. A nurse entered the room, rubbing hand sanitizer up his arms. "We did everything we could," he said with a tinge of sadness.

"I know," I groaned. And then, I signed the papers approving the required autopsy. Sometimes, I want to know more.

We had been married for twenty-five and a half years.

I was now something I had never wanted to be—a widow. The time from his prostate cancer diagnosis until his death from a heart attack was ten months.

I held no anger with Frank for "abandoning" me. The person who abandons someone makes a conscious choice to leave. Frank chose to live by consenting to the cardiac bypass. He did not choose to leave this life. Likewise, I felt no guilt about the events leading to his death. His health status resulted from his lifestyle decisions and the health changes he kept from his physician. Yet, I was saddened that his deeply internalized childhood fear of physicians and healthcare prevented him from admitting that he needed help or asking for help. He was never able to overcome that fear. I'm not sure he was even conscious of the connection.

The Early Days

I drove home by myself in the dark at 4:30 in the morning. Jaws clenched, I left voice messages for my sons as I left the hospital parking garage. I didn't want to talk to anyone while driving because I would fall apart with another ninety minutes to drive. Once home, I called my sister and notified Frank's girls. The girls asked about a burial service, and again, I had to dissuade them from coming because of COVID restrictions. Within hours, my sons arrived from their respective homes.

The hospital would not release Frank's body to the funeral home until after the autopsy. Given the overflow of COVID victims in morgues at that time, there was no way to know when the hospital would release his body. I called the morgue at least twice weekly for word of his release.

My sons attacked the heavy, heavy burden of removing Frank's accumulations. I would never have been able to parse all the items by myself. I would have been so overwhelmed by the number of Frank's collections that throwing a lit match into the house and walking out the door seemed reasonable. At my request, the boys started packing Frank's things and delivering them to Goodwill, a used bookstore, and other places. They had no connection to the ephemera, so they could dispatch the collections without sentiment. I curated items from Frank's collections to send to the girls.

While my sons filled boxes, I notified his science colleagues and the university where he taught. The scientists were distressed, not only by the loss of a colleague but also because of the loss of a great scientific mind. They bemoaned that he wouldn't be present to help study and learn about the COVID-19 virus. They commented on their belief that Frank would have solved the unknown.

On the second day, as the boys worked upstairs, I entered our bedroom and closed the door. I picked up Frank's pillow, smelled it, and screamed into it. I felt strangely unsatisfied, unsettled, and completely unreal. *I don't do this. Screaming into a pillow is not me. This isn't some romance novel. I solve problems. I don't fall apart.* I am a woman with a life story and resumé that acknowledges vast and varied experience, strength, control, wisdom, and no fear of confrontation when needed.

People have labeled me a "formidable woman." That woman would not scream into a pillow or act without a discernible purpose or value. That woman would control any emotion and do what needed to be done. I was disappointed in myself for what I perceived as pointless emotional behavior.

I was invincible . . . until I wasn't.

My younger son went home after three days. My older son's restaurant was closed, so he stayed for a month.

Three weeks after Frank's death, the morgue released his body. The funeral home representative had warned me that someone would have to identify him. The identification would probably be emotionally difficult because his body had changed. Since he was to be cremated, his body was not embalmed.

Identifying Frank's body was a task I could only ask myself to do. I did not want anyone else to have that vision as their last memory of Frank. Years earlier, my niece had knitted him a bright red winter scarf. He was so thrilled that she made the scarf just for him. I gave the scarf and some clothing to the funeral home. They included the scarf when they prepared his body for my identification. I focused on the scarf.

My older son had accompanied me to the funeral home, and while I thought he was in the hallway, he walked into the viewing room behind me. Later, I asked him to tell me about his experience. Was he shocked to see Frank's body? He said he was not shocked because the body looked just as it was supposed to look. He continued, "Just because the body looked as it did, it didn't change my thoughts or perspectives about Frank as a good, gentle, kind man."

Perhaps my protective thoughts were more about not giving people enough credit to hold or make their own perspectives. I am unsure about this. Was I not crediting people for their strength because I was grieving? Or was I acting out of the stoicism ingrained in my life history? What was I protecting them from?

I made the decision not to have any service for Frank. The primary reason was that I knew I couldn't handle interacting with others. I did not want to be accountable to the social construct that, as a grieving widow, I extend my psychic energy to the presence of others. I chose to protect myself by withdrawing. I did not miss any of the advertised social benefits of a public funeral service. And I certainly wasn't beholden to the idea that I owed "a community" the public venue of a funeral service to showcase grief. My brain and nervous system needed me to withdraw. COVID funeral service restrictions provided cover for my decision.

As the first month passed, my older son went back home. I took up permanent residence on my sofa with my new friend, Netflix. My new friend did not require thinking or feeling and very little physical activity. Netflix was forgiving and held no judgments about me, my experience, and my intermittent showering. Netflix was the technological "proof of life" that required nothing from me.

Frank and I had multiple "what-if" conversations about our potential deaths throughout our twenty-five years of marriage. We had all the appropriate paperwork to make life easier for the surviving spouse. Frank feared money; I became our money handler and financial planner. We had built a significant financial cushion to support either of us. We thought we knew all we needed to transition to the status of widow/widower.

Then, unexpected financial shocks started hitting me. Frank's Social Security and government retirement money did not arrive. At this point, I learned that Social Security and the federal government stop all payments once a death is reported. Despite my immediate attention to having them transferred into my name, it would be nine stressful months before the funds started again. Fortunately, I had the financial resources to endure that nine-month delay.

The repeated stress of follow-up phone calls and due diligence impacted my health and patience. I struggled to be my "normal" self and to maintain my photography and art studio. I am astounded to go through my files and see client sessions I do not remember.

A caring colleague asked me to assist him with a family photography session. The session would be conducted at the client's home. Thinking it would be good for me to step into the world, I agreed. As I followed my GPS direction, the streets started feeling familiar. It seemed I had seen these homes before. As I drove through neighborhoods, I felt a déjà vu that came with a sidecar of nausea. My hands started shaking on the steering wheel. My arms felt numb. I reached the client's home and tried to help set up the lighting equipment. Abruptly, I realized the directions to this home were the same roads and neighborhoods I had driven to take Frank to the regional medical center. The client's home was mere blocks from the medical center. My vision clouded, and my heart rate increased to the point I couldn't breathe. All the sounds and voices around me were muffled. I was having a full-blown panic attack. I told my colleague I had to leave and drove home.

As I pulled away from the home, I retrieved some knowledge about how my body works. I knew I could slow my heart rate by holding my breath—which should have been easy since I couldn't get my breath. I started a count: one short breath in, hold for one, one short breath out, short hold for one; in, hold, out, hold, in, hold, out, hold, one, one, one, one, one. Over the miles, I increased to a two-count, then a three-count, then a four-count. My heart rate gradually slowed. The closer I got to home, the more my panic attack receded.

How did I get home safely? It was probably divine intervention because I don't know. I don't remember. All I know is I had to leave that area immediately. Once I got home, I sat on the sofa in a stupor for the rest of the evening.

I participated in educational efforts but did not have the energy or focus to continue. I struggled to attend community groups. I lost patience with people who wasted my time and energy, so I left those groups.

I hated the question from people who knew Frank had prostate cancer, "How is Frank doing?" When delivering the answer, I felt neither the desire nor the internal energy to soothe other people's discomfort about death. I did not need to expand upon the hard fact. I bluntly responded, in a flat voice, "he's dead," then turned and walked away. Eventually, I could soften my response to "Thank you for asking. He's dead." I needed no other conversation about his death, and the question would lead to stories I didn't need to recount repeatedly.

While my grief manifested as my need to isolate and inability to hold a mental focus, two superb punsters I know tangentially were daily lights for me. Their daily social media posts made me laugh—every day. I was able to thank both for the small cheer they gave me daily. Look for laughter—it's not wrong to laugh during grief. Laughter is healing, even for the briefest of moments.

Brain fog became a constant companion. A brain that constantly processes, analyzes, and creates new information suddenly became dormant. The brain that had been my distinction, safe space, and survival mode was a blank, dark wall. I lost connection with a lot of information that had helped me previously. My knowledge of how the brain functions during trauma escaped me. A black hole in my memory swallowed and lost information within two seconds of hearing it. I wish I had known my memory would be so unreliable. This unreliable memory would come back to haunt me in a big way. I learned to take a "second set of ears" for important meetings. This person would take notes for me, so I had the information available at later dates.

This, Too, Shall Pass

As difficult as the circumstances surrounding Frank's death, never-ending paperwork, brain fog, and inability to venture outside my deliberate isolation were, I knew it to be a time-limited process.

My earlier divorce did prepare me for Frank's death. I knew I could come out of this morass of grief. I knew I could live by myself again, and the trauma cycle would eventually yield to a fully lived and appreciated life. Once again, life ended one cycle, so a new path in life could begin.

While I did fall into the deep dark hole of brain fog and existential crisis, I did not lie in my bed trembling. I did not lose my sanity to anger. I did not doubt my abilities would become clear and focused again. I did not employ negative self-talk about being a widow in grief—my grief. I never doubted that I deserved to live a happy life.

The Firsts

Our birthdays were six months apart, his on the twenty-fifth, mine on the twenty-sixth. We celebrated "half-birthdays," meaning we each celebrated two birthdays every year. Half-birthdays were just a cute way to rejoice with each other. His birthday came two months and three days after his death. I had no major breakdown. I had successfully filed the "event" in the archives much quicker than usual. It was his birthday, but he wasn't present. There was nothing to be done.

Thanksgiving rolled up on the calendar, the first big family event after his death. I traveled to spend the day with my younger son and his family. Truthfully, I don't remember much about that holiday. I do remember one of my grandsons mentioning, "Grandpa Frank died." I knew, as a six-year-old, he didn't know what "died" meant, but his comment set his parents to shushing him.

My sister invited me to her house for a family Christmas, but I declined. Even after the invitation was proffered several times, I repeatedly declined. I just did not have the energy to travel and be with people. Yes, they were people who loved and cared for me, but I was unable to expend that energy. I suspect I spent Christmas watching holiday movies on Netflix.

As the first anniversary of Frank's death approached, I began preparing to sell our house. The most relevant thing about this anniversary was that I had lived through the first year. It seems a small win, but I celebrate that win. I kept myself alive.

Time to Move

After the first year, COVID-19 was still active, and the housing market went over the top. Given how rapidly houses were selling, finding a new home from afar was impossible. My sister and brother-in-law graciously consented to my living with them while I hunted for a house. I moved back to Ohio, closer to my sister and older son.

I sold my home and nearly everything I owned at the time. I planned to start anew as much as possible. As the day to move came closer, I felt a surprising and unexplained anger toward the house I had lived in for over thirty years. I loved this house. I had worked to make it my house. As I left the driveway for the final time, I said to the house, "I'm done with you." With the help of the Karens and my son, I packed the remaining items and moved back to Ohio.

I found a new home within three days and moved in six months later when the building was complete. It was now sixteen months after Frank's death.

Self-Isolation

The new house became my aversion therapy. I didn't have to think as long as I was decorating and building cabinets, closets, and a mudroom; installing shiplap, wainscoting, and crown moldings; replacing flooring; and hanging wallpaper. I was comfortable as long as I kept myself busy. I created my new safe space. Netflix, the sofa, and I continued our long-term relationship.

I was comfortable not interacting with my new neighbors. I did wave when I saw them, but consciously working to establish friendly conversations was impossible.

The inability to remember (or maybe the accountant didn't tell me) returned to bite me at tax time. I had assumed that tax withholding would automatically continue when Frank's retirement funds were transferred into my name. No, it did not. Knowledge about tax withholding was another gap in the preparations we had constructed.

I had gone an entire year without paying income tax, and my tax bill that year was a whopping $12,000. Again, I was fortunate enough to have the funds to pay the bill. Yet, I was stunned that my accountant did not tell me (as far as I remembered) to ensure tax withholding started again. I should have taken a "second set of ears" to that meeting after Frank's death.

Health

There is no cure for being human. The body has a mind of its own. If the brain turns away from the trauma, the body speaks the truth in its language—the language of unstable health. The body will express grief in its own way.

During Frank's prostate cancer treatments, my blood pressure shot up. The more I fought for clarity from his physicians, the more I could feel intense pressure in the back of my skull. The self-help techniques that had been effective no longer worked. I had to go on medication. After Frank died, my heart rhythm became erratic. For an entire year, I experienced bigeminal premature ventricular contractions (PVCs), causing my heart to pump less blood and oxygen due to every other heartbeat occurring early, preventing my heart ventricles from filling fully. I experienced frequent episodes of PVCs running together that had the potential to be fatal. The cardiologist, who specialized in electrical heart problems, exerted no effort to determine the cause of this potentially life-threatening arrhythmia. He didn't seem at all interested in me, my grief, or my heart. He only cared that I was seventy years old—an "old woman"—despite my usually active lifestyle.

I have high expectations of the healthcare system. I'm frequently disappointed.

I became increasingly depressed—who wouldn't with ever-decreasing oxygen levels circulating through the body? The only treatments my physicians offered for PVCs were "black box warning" drugs. That is to say, the drug carries a significant risk of severe side effects, even life-threatening adverse effects.

Yes, I have a love/hate relationship with the healthcare system, especially as I grow older. I hate ageism in healthcare.

While I missed Frank dearly, crying would not bring him back nor make my heart beat correctly. If I did cry, I was alone with Netflix and my tears. The crying always resulted from some stupid commercial or scene in a movie. According to some people, however, I did not behave as emotionally as they wanted me to. The fact that I isolated myself and was physiologically depressed "didn't count" as emotional enough in their expectations. The isolation and depression were not visible to those looking in. And yet, I am a "practical griever." My practical grieving process wholly aligned with my "just the facts, ma'am" demeanor.

A romantic notion of grief is love with no place to go. My logical brain can't accept this analogy as based on reality. My love for Frank did not dissipate. While he is no longer here physically, I have untold numbers of memories that I hold tenderly. My affection is present in those memories. And yes, some memories are more poignant than others. My love exists in those memories. My active remembering, my mode of remembrance, is the recognition of our years together. My memories are as prayers of gratitude for Frank.

Bring on the Woo

Before Frank's death, I was an avid reader of two to three books per week. Other than the new publications from my favorite author, I was unable or had no desire to read.

I was finally focusing enough to read another book. In a magical coincidence, I found the book *Dying to Be Me* by Anita Moorjani. Anita had a near-death experience. In her profound spiritual awakening, she viewed the tapestry of her life and the threads of people who had entered and left it.

Suddenly, Frank's death had context other than fact. The tapestry of his life was complete. His completed tapestry allowed me to continue, eventually creating an extended life of adventure and wonder woven into my own life tapestry.

At that very moment, I also understood my cardiac problems were related to "broken heart syndrome." My heart was speaking the truth of my loss. This sudden realization was one of those pieces of information I knew professionally but had been unable to access for my own sake. I knew how to fix this, and my bigeminy stopped within forty-eight hours. The awareness of what was happening brought me back to a normal cardiac rhythm. While my body had healed, my spirit felt as lifeless as a wet paper bag.

Puppy Depression

Gradually, the voice of the problem-solving woman started to drop hints into my consciousness. "Get up and get outside. Walk, do something," she said. I decided the best way up and out was to get a dog. If I had to walk a dog once or twice daily, I would pull myself out of my inertia.

Again, coincidence struck as a neighbor had eight golden retriever puppies that needed homes. I had raised several puppies through the years and felt confident I had the energy for a new puppy. I severely overestimated my current physical energy for puppy training and deeply underestimated how much power a golden retriever puppy has. My depression worsened because I felt powerless against the furry land shark. A puppy was like having a newborn with razors for teeth. I did not sleep uninterrupted for over four months. Worse, I began to doubt my decision and felt the dog would be better cared for if I rehomed him. I knew if I gave up on the puppy, I would be unable to forgive myself. I would quit the dog because I had failed. The answer was to retrain me.

I created a retraining plan for myself, and it worked. I had to retrain myself to be aware of puppy signals. I had to reduce the space I gave the puppy in the house. He was too young to understand the whole house was not his potty space. I had to accept that I couldn't trust this baby canine to make good decisions. I was the one who had to make good decisions. I was the one who had to exert the energy to focus near-constant attention on him and his behaviors/needs. I was the one who had to move more quickly and get off the sofa sooner.

The dog is now a cuddle bug. Even though he is the best of boys, rescuing a senior dog would have been easier for me at the time. Yet, he has served my purpose of "getting out of myself." Everyone loves a puppy, and our daily walks opened me to engaging and making friends with neighbors. Most people in the neighborhood now know Augie, the golden retriever walking with the white-haired woman. And it's easier for me to talk to them as they talk to the dog.

Existential Crisis—Dark Night of the Soul

My lowest point was darker and more confusing. My grief manifested as my natural inclination to sequester myself and not expend valuable brain calories with others. I came out of the brain fog just enough to understand that I was puzzled, distressed, and further depressed by my inability to take action other than walking the dog, sitting on the sofa, and watching Netflix. I felt stripped of energy as if my bone marrow had vanished with no way to replenish it.

Why couldn't I be the woman who took action? I felt bound in darkness. Even more unacceptable and frightening was that I had no grand vision or dreams. I had a void where creativity and ambitions dwelt. I could not see a desired future against what I was living. The black wall was too dense.

I did not recognize this woman. I could not accept the differences between the woman I had been and the woman I now was. I could not solve this crisis. I was incapable of thinking my way out—which made me angry. The anger at myself deepened the depression. Was I at a point of no return? How should I move forward? Could I move forward?

Over the months, I gradually questioned and analyzed many aspects of my childhood traumas. What was it about those traumas, combined with my neurodivergence, that brought me to my survival structure of self-isolation? And the answer was abandonment.

The Beginning of Me

My father was a man ahead of his time. He was an electrician and had seen his share of coworkers killed or maimed in electrical accidents. After visiting a young widow with three children under the age of five, he came home and told my mother that he didn't care what she did, but she would get a job and learn to take care of herself and her three kids. If the job required schooling, they would find a way to pay for it. My mother became a licensed practical nurse.

He taught my younger sister and brother and me how to make household repairs. He was adamant that my sister and I would be able to care for ourselves. We learned the correct (and safe) way to change out electrical outlets. He gave each of us a toolbox with tools. We were proficient in the use of power tools. The two of us helped him put a roof on the new home he was building. We learned to change the oil and tires on our cars before he released us to the open roads.

When we reached sixteen, he bought us a piece of fine jewelry. His purpose was to teach us that we each deserved a partner who would value us as much as he did. My sister chose wisely when it came to a partner. Me? I didn't choose wisely the first time.

For all his insights about how to prepare us for the future, there were two areas he refused to talk about: finances and preparations for our parents' inevitable deaths. He was of a generation that didn't speak of these inevitabilities. His inability to discuss them was a great motivator for me. I learned how to handle and grow money. And in my future career as an intensive care nurse, I focused on death and dying.

I have to analyze and synthesize information before I can know and respond to emotion. My dearest friend of fifty years described me as the "just the facts, ma'am, just the facts" woman. How my emotions manifest as an adult is not what others expect.

I never learned to live with fear. I replaced fear with anger because there was control in anger. My childhood interactions with my mother taught me that the safest place to be was "in my head." It was safer to stay solitary and withdrawn.

As the eldest child, I was born out of expectation. My mother had chosen to become pregnant while a senior in high school. She reasoned that she would have nothing if my father (soon to be deployed to Korea) were killed. Thus, she would have something of him if she had a baby. I had a role to fill for her.

And yet, she was used to being abandoned as a child, and those abandonments carried over into her own life with me. She contracted polio, and my grandparents removed me from her until she was no longer infectious. Over the following years, she was hospitalized frequently for various illnesses. Migraine headaches sequestered her in her bedroom for six years. And when she did come out of her room, she was vicious in words and actions. Other abandonments were threatened through letters and silence.

Yet, we were raised to show only stoicism and what was a false nobility—the romantic and naive vision of chivalry. We were those who would be willing to give our lives for others. We were to be the protectors of others. We were expected to always do the "right thing." We were to be paragons of moral excellence—which came with heavy touches of disdain and distrust of others. Such a heavy burden for a ten-year-old child to grasp and carry, yet this ten-year-old girl didn't realize the burden was unreasonable! At age ten, I became the de facto caretaker of my sister, four and a half years younger, and my baby brother, nine years my junior.

When I was sixteen, my mother stepped out of her darkened bedroom and back into our daily lives. All hell broke loose between us when my mother tried to reassert her maternal power over me. The dangerous state of cognitive dissonance reared itself in my head, realizing what was expected of me and, later, my siblings was not being modeled for us. My anger at this deception was palpable and vehement.

One of our fights involved me standing defiantly across the kitchen from her and telling her, "You can beat me all you want. You can lock me in my room. You can throw me out of the house. But you will never break my spirit." She looked at me with recognition in her eyes. Maybe she had this same stand-off with her father?

The fights between us intensified and fortified my natural need for isolation.

My mother shot down my desire to become a physician. In her words, I was too weak. I later discovered that she had aspired to become a doctor and earned a full scholarship from one of the Seven Sisters Colleges. (The Seven Sisters were colleges that provided equivalent Ivy League education to women.) She feared feeling shame if the other girls knew her father was an alcoholic. It never occurred to her the other girls might have their own fears or alcoholic fathers. Additionally, she would not have to go to college if she was pregnant. My embryonic self saved her a second time.

In my mid-adult years, Mom admitted that she had been afraid of me. She was angry that everything I accomplished, everything I attempted, reminded her of her own personal choices and the resulting unsatisfactory consequences. She didn't understand how my brain worked, and thus, she simultaneously feared me and was angry with me. She feared my ability to see and hear things few people can. As we grew older, her jealousy, fear, and insecurity became a toxic brew directed toward my "different brain."

Weeks before she died, my mother apologized and said she tried hard to be a good mother. She knew she had missed the mark most of the time. I was with her as she died. It was only the two of us as I came into the world. It was only the two of us as she left the world.

You may wonder why this childhood history is relevant to my experience as a new widow. What seems to be obvious now is the revelation of how deeply ingrained experiences and behaviors developed in childhood stayed with me. In retrospect, I was stunned to be so affected by Frank's death. My sister and I have joked that we are missing the compassion gene. I wasn't sure I could or would have these feelings until they pulled me asunder. Perhaps I do have the compassion gene, even for myself.

And even though my childhood was "not normal," what I know is that my mother was a deeply scarred child buried inside an adult body. The wounded mother of the mid-twentieth century did not have access to mental healthcare or the understanding of childhood traumas as we do today. And yet . . . here I am. I had to acknowledge my past to live into my future.

I hadn't considered the remaining impacts of my childhood relative to Frank's death. And yet, it was obvious to me the decisions Frank made in his last days were based on his childhood experiences and contributed to his death. I suspect we all carry those remnants of childhood that influence how we live through trauma. Maybe we're not immediately conscious of them or believe, as I did, that we have overcome those experiences.

If I changed my survival structure, then it should follow that behavioral changes would occur. The company of my sister, brother-in-law, and the Karens provided incremental changes. I had to manage the tension of self-isolation against my current ability to envision a change. If I could control the strain between my inertia and a need for selective community interaction, I could break down the dark wall and see the light again. Slowly, I stepped out.

During the mornings, I would stand on my deck and watch wild rabbits and deer munch grasses at the forested edge of my backyard. I would take in the golden morning sun as it eased across the forest. One morning, I noticed I was smiling. And I was pleased to realize the smile had come into being on its own. I felt . . . happy.

The Turn-Around

I have my sister and her husband to thank for starting my movement out of my existential crisis. They invited me to attend an exercise class at the local YMCA. We met in a gym two days a week with thirty other people. Objective #1? Be around other people while grounded by the presence of my sister and brother-in-law. Objective #2? Move my body and work my way back to a healthier state.

The Karens

The Karens and I were acquaintances who traveled in the same business circles. The trip to Morocco was a longer exposure to each other than ever before. I experienced extreme car sickness during our road travels, and Tall Karen was kind enough to offer me her anti-nausea bands. She had empathy for my car sickness. Since meeting in Morocco, we have organized several trips together. Each of us has a unique skill that contributes to the smoothness of our travels. Tall Karen enjoys driving and is our designated driver. Short Karen is eager to experience everything, so she plans detailed itineraries. As for me, I handle the dishes and am the Big Thinker.

Frank passed away in March of the year following our Morocco trip. Since the Karens were not aware of my neurodivergence, they interpreted my need for solitude as a sign that I needed help. They came up with a plan to assist me based on their beliefs about how I was dealing with my grief. (I've teased them that they were working from incomplete data.) I was unaware of their plan and only learned about it two years later during one of our annual trips. As fellow widows, they understood the lack of energy that prohibits the "call me if you need anything."

I value solitude, so building a strong friendship with anyone takes time and numerous interactions. My process of forming a deep friendship can be likened to the developmental stages of an infant. It starts with the seed being sown, and a "baby friendship" is born. Similar to how a child progresses through developmental stages, such as learning to crawl, walk, and talk, my friendships progress through developmental stages of mutual trust, respect, and emotional intimacy.

Writing our book was similar to cultivating our friendship, as both went through different stages of development. Juggling the effort to build and sustain friendships while navigating through the stages of writing a book was quite demanding for us. It often felt like we were nurturing two fledgling projects simultaneously. There were moments when the phases of our friendship and the stages of our book collided.

I value the Karens' friendship. When we trust and respect each other, we bring light, joy, and creativity into each other's lives. Interacting with just two Karens is the perfect size for my nervous system to handle.

The invitations from my sister and brother-in-law and the plans of the Karens have affirmed the importance of friends while I navigated through my widowhood process. Friends and family have been vital for my transformation, health, and progress.

Selective Outings

I opened up and felt willing to experience more opportunities and adventures. I chose four monthly events: a book club, Ladies' Night, and two local Chambers of Commerce. Four interactions during a month limited the number of people I interacted with and preserved my energy levels. Even though I stepped out to these events, I limit my exposure to other people because their energies are an assault on my nervous system. Recently, I chose to discontinue my Chamber of Commerce activities because there were too many people and too much noise.

My choice to engage more often will be determined by what changes I seek and my need to conserve my psychic stamina. I will choose those affairs that lead me to be more of myself or intrigue me. I will take on new adventures. I will become more of the expansive me. I do and will continue to exercise my version of radical self-care, which includes my need for solitude. And I will do all these things on my schedule.

Transformation

The unexpected death of Frank was akin to being thrown through a door into the unknown. I oscillated between processing loss and preparing for other life changes as I grew through this trauma response. Grief is a portal into transformation. My transformation began the moment I became a widow; I just might not have been aware of it. Whether it was a conscious thought or a thought pushed to the side in the early days, I asked, "Who do I want to be now?"

Years ago, in my master's program in community health nursing, I had to write a theory of Impaired Health. I built my theory around the changes in the self of the grieving survivor. I wrote of the role of the deceased spouse's input or contributions to the fullness of self of the remaining partner. As I passed through the timeline of my grief, I understood at the cellular level (as we would say in nursing) that Frank had impacted my self-identity. I felt safe, protected, and known. Our respective neurodivergence gave us the space to be ourselves without judgment.

Transformation in widowhood for me was showing up in the world in new ways. And as healing occurs by degrees, so too does transformation. It involved finding a new meaning or a more profound respect for my life. My transformation has been the healing of my life and a creative process that eventually produced levels of wholeness, grace, and beauty.

But my transformation was not just cerebral. My journey through the existential crisis was not a psychological problem; it was a spiritual reckoning. I experienced the dark night of the soul. My dark night was an experience that had to be examined and understood as the progression of my own self-realization. I could not reason my way back to health and action. My forces of reason, logic, and mind were broken down. I was experiencing a crisis of powerlessness where circumstances seemed more powerful than me. I had to answer, "What does it mean to know my inner self while knowing I cannot change the characteristics of my neurodivergence? Where does my power lie?"

It seems that in many of our medical establishments, we have lost the spirit in the Mind-Body-Spirit connection. We recognize the death of a spouse as a major stressor in life, yet that stressor is most often viewed through only the lenses of the mind and body. The inevitable painful transitions of life automatically draw us into an interior process of evaluation. If we only focus on our mind or body, we may miss the chance to create meaningful new directions in our lives. These new directions can result in greater empathy, creativity in our choices and actions, and a greater map of what life can be.

I walked through the dark night toward the light while reflecting on my childhood, engaging in internal dialogue and contemplation, and employing my need for solitude. This process was about forgiveness for my mother and for myself. There was no way to avoid this hard, heart-wrenching work—it was the point of no return. My healing required struggling through emotional pain and uncertainty. This healing required pulling the dusty childhood memories from my mental archive, reread-ing them, and analyzing, processing, and synthesizing myself into a healthier and stronger woman.

Transformation taught me the most about who I am and who I can become.

My transformation changed how I saw myself and my psychology. I realized a more profound capacity to appreciate my life. My transfor-mation expressed gratitude for the past and excitement for the future. Most often, I recognized this shift in retrospect. I often only recognized my transformation process in hindsight when clarity brought forth the realization. By transforming myself, hopefully, I will not transmit the fears that burdened my mother, her fears that influenced my develop-ment. Yet, her fears and insecurities contributed to who I am.

Eighteen years earlier, the Buddhist monk had told me, "Your heart is weary." At the time, I performed a mental checkmark: "Weary heart, check. Yeah. Look into this sometime." Frank's death was the catalyst that forced me into a deep exploration of why my heart was weary (and erratic). His death was the event I could not "put a mental checkmark by" and keep going. His death was the event that brought me to a physi-cal and emotional stop.

What did that mean in those intervening eighteen years? Frank had been a salve for my weariness. There was peace, respect, support, comfort, and understanding. I had no need to struggle against physical or psychic energy losses. Now that he was no longer present, what did I need to do to rest or restore this weary heart? I had no choice but to live as quietly as possible in order to accomplish my needed healing.

Back to Art

I fell back into my creativity, looking for beauty. I find a solace, an anchoring of my soul in appreciating or creating beauty. I experience the flow and melding into something other, bigger than myself. I receive wisdom when I create art.

I wandered through the neighborhood, taking experimental pictures of flowering trees, weeds, and railroad tracks. My art journal contains descriptions of "Shattered Tranquility," a photographic portrait of multiple reflections of me in a shattered mirror. "Digging Out" was inspired by the weeping willow in my sister's backyard. I described digging myself out of the earth under the willow. I searched for things that inspired me, whether through people, nature, animals, or art. I made a decision to find and appreciate something valuable in my life every day and cherish it for the entire day.

In hindsight, I realized that creating art brought peace to my heart and spirit. Despite my brain-fogged condition, my quiet but persistent spirit drove me to create awe and beauty. My spirit was directing a movement to rest my weary heart. My utter sense of powerlessness and lack of energy allowed my spirit to quietly take control of my healing journey.

The artistic additions I built into my new home were the physical embodiment of creativity. Yes, the physical work occupied my body and mind, but under the surface of paint and power tools was the unrecognized anchoring of my soul in awe and beauty in my new home—my new sanctuary. My return to art reminded me that we, as humans, have the capacity to rise again and step into a different life.

And now, I am accompanying my neighbors through the journey of death and widowhood. I find myself to be remarkably centered. I may be calm, but my grief has been triggered. Not only do I empathize with new widows, but I also recall my own loss, which has cultivated this empathy. However, this grief will only linger for a few days, unlike the many months it originally consumed.

I am walking a journey with these new widows that reinforces that all our stories of loss and grief are connected and all our hard-fought wisdom demands to be shared. That particular wisdom honors the universality of the life-death experience. And in that universality, we find help, guidance, support, and growth.

It would be sad if I, as a widow, resisted the insights into the cracks of my being presented by Frank's death. The light is useful in healing; it allows me to see myself and others to see a part of me.

Writing this book is a way to move forward after Frank's death. It's not about finding meaning in Frank's death. There is no particular meaning to his death other than we live and die. It is the way of life, pure and simple. My interactions within the world aim to share my experiences and offer hope to other widows and their loved ones.

Our stories of shared experience weave us together. The tapestry of our connections has been there; we just haven't experienced that 360-degree view of its size, scope, colors, and design until we realize all our transformations are woven from rugged and painful life events. We have the option and ability to take steps into our new future.

◘   ◘   ◘

Short Insights

These brief insights, born from our collective journey through grief, offer a glimpse into what we've learned, what we've done, and how we've coped. They serve as concise answers to the challenges faced by those who have recently been widowed.

There is no one way to grieve. Our individual stories presented three different versions of grieving. Each was effective, meeting the widow's needs and sparking growth and healing.

Be realistic. Your energy levels may come and go. You may be fired up one moment and exhausted the next. Just know this is a normal process during grief. Listen to your body and take the breaks you need to restore yourself.

Social expectations of the widow. You have the power to decide whether to go along with any traditional social expectations after losing your spouse. This might include arranging a public service or sending thank-you notes to those who offered their condolences. If doing these things brings you comfort, go ahead and do them. But if they feel like too much to handle, it's completely okay to put your well-being first and ignore these social expectations. Take care of yourself.

Asking for help. Upsetting changes require us to adjust our thinking and behavior. As widows, we may experience brain fog for a short or long period of time, resulting in difficulty making decisions. It's important to ask friends or family to support you by being a second set of ears during important meetings. Sometimes, it's easy for us not to ask for help as we don't want to burden anyone or simply lack the energy to do so. Remember, you have family, friends, and neighbors who would love to help you; they might not know how to help. Don't hesitate to ask for what you need.

Go for it. If you want to try something new, ignore your self-doubts and go for it.

Paperwork challenges. The paperwork can be overwhelming. You don't have to do it all at once. Prioritize by importance, and work on it a bit at a time. Ask for help from someone knowledgeable.

Friendship. Some friends fall away, and some step up. Let those who fall away go gently; lean into the ones who come forward for you.

Make social plans in advance. You're more likely to follow through, even if you can only stay for five minutes.

Be prepared that your money may not be immediately available. Financial security should be a top priority from the beginning of your marriage. Consider establishing a relationship with an accountant or finding a trustworthy financial advisor to help you navigate your financial journey together. Build a financial cushion to cover all your expenses until retirement funds and Social Security start flowing again. Please refer to the next section for additional tips on preparing for financial security.

Anger is real. When you're angry, your body needs to release energy. Try taking a fast walk or screaming into a pillow to release the energy.

Protecting others. Be aware of holding things in because you want to protect others by not sharing difficult information or moments. When the loss of a spouse rocks your life, you might be inclined to build a fence around your feelings and thoughts. We learned that we often did not give others enough credit to manage the tough stuff. We also learned that sometimes our subconscious was trying to protect ourselves instead. There are other reasons to share the tough stuff. We explain why in Part Three.

Waiting a year. Not every widow can wait a year to make a big decision like selling a home or a business. Those decisions must be made according to the widow's immediate circumstances. Consult your financial advisors about the best course of action. Take those "universal suggestions" with a grain of salt.

Grief is not a "one-and-done" process. Grief morphs and ultimately does not continue to be an ever-present companion, but it still lives within us. The following illustrations show how grief is like a supersized balloon. As the intensity of your trauma recedes, the grief balloon slowly deflates, but it can still "bounce around" with your emotions.

Trigger events. Over time, your grief balloon may only be triggered by certain events, such as anniversaries, weddings, and graduations. You never know what the trigger will be or when it will hit. Recognize it as part of the healing process.

"Grief never ends, but it changes.
It's a passage, not a place to stay."
—Queen Elizabeth I

The Grief Response Over Time

In the early stage of widowhood, the effect of trauma is so intense that it constantly hits the button of grief.

As the intensity of the trauma lessens over time, the button of grief is triggered less often.

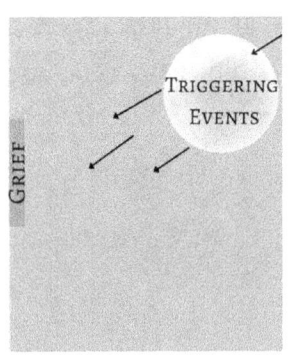

Years later, events such as anniversaries can trigger a grief response.

Adapted from Lauren Herschel, TWITTER December 2017. Used with permission.

◙   ◙   ◙

PART TWO

Mamas,
Teach Your Daughters
to Be Widows

Illustration: The topics that worried our survey respondents the most.

How Every Wife Should Be Prepared

While preparing this book, we spoke to dozens of other widows to collect their advice, insights, and what they wished they had known. Surprisingly, many of them shared that their own mothers had been widows for twenty-five to forty years but had never spoken about their experience. We discovered that a lot of these women were unprepared for the crisis that hits when you lose a spouse. Even those who had thought they had planned well were surprised by some of the challenges they encountered.

During one of our conversations, Rebecca declared, "I think we need to tell women, 'Mamas, teach your daughters to be widows!'" She was right. Women should spend time soon after marriage preparing for the unpalatable concept of being alone and widowed.

Although the suggestions below are designed to create preparedness for widowhood, they are immediately beneficial, practical, and critical to making your life easier. They build independence, self-confidence, and the comfort of being prepared for anything coming your way.

You will need a way to keep track of the "who, what, where, and how" of each topic below—whether for yourself, your spouse, or your loved ones. The workbook *I Didn't See That Coming* by Karen Smith Racicot (Tall Karen) was created for this purpose after the death of her husband. The worksheets allow you to keep all of the pertinent information of your legal, financial, and insurance documents, as well as your assets, liabilities, passwords, and professional advisors. You will find more information about this workbook and how to order one in the "Resources" section of this book.

A checklist for being prepared is available through our website, *www.threewidows.com*. This checklist includes items to consider well before becoming a widow.

Legal Documents

According to Kiplinger Finance, a support network of experts who can help a new widow can be just as important as your personal support network at such a difficult time.

Legal documents are designed to convey your wishes when a life event happens. Without these documents, your loved ones can't make certain decisions about your health; there may be unforeseen tax consequences, your partner or heirs might not inherit what you think they will, or your kids may not be raised by whom you want.

Contact an estate planning lawyer to help you prepare the essential legal documents. Visit a lawyer for the requirements in your state of residence, as each state may differ.

Below are some of the basic documents for estate planning. This is not a totally inclusive list, and not everyone will need all the documents.

Will

According to a 2020 Gallup survey, about 54 percent of U.S. citizens do not have a will that contains instructions for distributing their finances, assets, or caregiving of children, nor a living will for their medical directives.

Write a will immediately after marriage. This is the heart of your estate. Even if you are newly married with a rental apartment and two cars, you need a simple will. You want to ensure you can transfer all your properties and assets appropriately and easily.

As the marriage progresses, bank accounts, retirement funds, houses, cars, and furniture accumulate. Ensure they are titled correctly (typically in both spouses' names) for easy transitions. One woman reported that her adult stepchildren came into her home after her husband died and took most of the furniture. They claimed the furnishings were "heirlooms" and belonged to their family.

Medical Directive, Medical and Financial Power of Attorney, Advanced Healthcare Directive (Living Will)

Create these documents before you need them. It is complex and may be impossible to obtain the appropriate paperwork during a spouse's illness or after their death. Some businesses, insurance companies, and banks may require financial power of attorney to pay, transfer, or assign the funds to you. Without powers of attorney for healthcare, medical professionals will make treatment decisions that may not match the wishes of you or your spouse.

Healthcare Insurance

Does your health insurance depend on your spouse's job? Will their insurance continue to cover you after their death? Is there a minimum number of years your spouse must work to maintain insurance coverage? For example, as a government employee, Frank had to work for five years to ensure that his insurance covered both himself and Rebecca for healthcare into his retirement years. As Frank's spouse, Rebecca's insurance coverage continued after his death.

If you are unsure about the answers to these questions, it is crucial to proactively determine what kind of healthcare coverage you will have in the event of his passing. By investigating other healthcare options that are available to you, you can be prepared and in control. The time to investigate is before you learn you no longer have coverage and have to scramble to purchase insurance.

Trusts

Trusts are legal documents that take care of special circumstances and are not required by everyone. Some examples may be to determine how assets flow in the event of a second marriage, distribute assets differently than what can be stated in the will, or help minimize taxes. Your lawyer will be able to advise you if a trust is a good option for your situation.

Finances

Our survey respondents' main concern was, "Do I have enough money?" They were worried about possible income loss or changes in benefit payments. They often lacked details about investments, insurance, debts, and various financial commitments. In some cases, their spouse managed all the finances, leaving them to figure everything out on their own.

This is where having important "what-if" conversations is invaluable. You and your spouse can discuss options in case of different life events, and make a plan for potential loss of income or additional expenses. These conversations will also help each spouse become more familiar with their current and future financial situations.

How Will Your Income Change?

Statistically, household income will drop by approximately 40 percent after the spouse's death. Yet, household expenses will typically drop by only 10 percent. Fifty-one percent of widows over sixty-five survive on less than $22,000 annually. (WISER: Women's Institute for a Secure Retirement.)

Financial self-care is protecting your future by collecting information. For example, if your spouse dies, what happens to his pension or retirement income? If you're both drawing Social Security, you will only be able to draw one after his death, which will significantly affect your income. Do you or should you have life insurance to cover the gap? Be sure to update or add to it as family and income levels change.

Based on our personal experiences, we recommend that every woman has enough money to cover up to nine months of expenses after her spouse dies. Build a financial cushion so you will be prepared if or when insurance or retirement monies arrive later than expected.

Beneficiaries, Deeds, and Titles

Ensure the beneficiaries are correct on all investment and retirement accounts and life insurance policies. Financial advisors and insurance agents estimate that 5 percent of all benefits go to the wrong person, typically an ex-spouse.

Also, ensure that you are named on the title of your house's deed and on your vehicles as appropriate.

Be Involved and Proactive in Your Finances

Other issues mentioned were the ability to trust insurance companies and financial advisors. Be sure to include yourself in conversations and interactions with your professional advisors. Not only will you be familiar with them, but you will also learn and keep current with the financial, legal, and insurance aspects affecting your life.

No one wants to think negatively of their spouse in the marriage. Yet, a few widows reported learning that their husbands had left them with huge debts and had cashed in all life insurance monies before death. One woman inherited a $4 million debt; another had an enormous deficit found in another state. For a few women, the spouse played on "romance" and gaslit the woman by suggesting she didn't "trust him." She was not to worry because he was taking care of everything. Each event happened because the spouse controlled and kept secrets about their financial state.

According to a May 2024 survey by the financial investment company Thrivent, 10 percent of widows were left with $100,000 in debt and 39 percent over $25,000 in debt. Seventy-one percent said that the loss of their spouse made paying off the debt moderately or much more difficult.

Your Credit Rating

Establish your own credit and obtain your own credit card independently of your spouse. If the spouse is the primary owner of the account, once you report his death, you will no longer have access to that card or the account, and may have difficulty establishing credit for yourself after his death. Be sure to have your name on the mortgage and car loan.

Have Those What-If Conversations

In one instance, the wife took care of all the finances, and conversations with her husband about money were totally transparent. However, they never talked about the future and didn't have any "what-if" conversations. When he died unexpectedly, she quickly reached the verge of bankruptcy based on their financial obligations and their lack of life insurance to cover them. She was confident in her financial awareness; they just never planned for something critical such as the husband's death.

Review What You Have

One suggestion from a financial advisor is to establish a quarterly or annual review of income and expenses, debts, assets, and investments. An in-depth review of all legal and financial paperwork, including beneficiaries, should be carried out after any significant life event or every five to seven years.

These reviews are critical to being prepared for unexpected life events. We have heard from multiple widows where an ex-wife was the beneficiary on life insurance and/or retirement accounts. Once your spouse dies, you are unable to change beneficiaries.

Example: One woman's name was not on the title of a house she purchased with her second husband. When he died unexpectedly and had significant debts, the lienholders took the house as payment. In addition, all the payouts from his life insurance and retirement were sent to his ex-wife because the beneficiaries on those documents weren't changed.

She was left with literally nothing.

Help Your Future Self by Getting Answers to These Questions as Soon as Possible:

- ✦ What institutions hold your money?

- ✦ Are your checking and savings accounts joint? Is a beneficiary or a "pay on death" arrangement made if the accounts are not jointly owned? Do you know how to access those accounts?

- ✦ Do you have investments? Where are they, and how can you access them?

- ✦ If one of you has a safety deposit box, do you know how to access it?

- ✦ Is your name on all joint property, such as your home?

These are all topics for you and your spouse to discuss together with your lawyer or financial advisor.

Business Owners

Are you a joint business owner? Do you have key person insurance for the business? Do you know who to call if it's your husband's business? If you both own the business, what do you want to do with it? How do you maintain your business life when your personal life falls apart? Do you have an employee or colleague to help distribute the workload? Be sure you understand the legal entity of the business and its ramifications. Preparation is key.

Passwords

Online financial and business transactions are ubiquitous. And that means every account has a username and a password. You need those usernames and passwords to access bank accounts, any household bills paid online, internet/cable services, streaming services, Wi-Fi, and the router. You must also access and close out social media, cell phone accounts, and subscriptions.

Your spouse may have had multiple professional accounts that must be closed. Rebecca's husband had three hundred cards with usernames and passwords for his professional accounts.

Create a Black Book for All of Your Passwords and Other Information

Consider building a Black Book. Construct spreadsheets and enter the passwords and other electronic IDs as they are developed. Slip the spreadsheet into plastic sleeves and put it into a binder. It is helpful to update the binder on an annual basis. Choose a yearly date that is meaningful to you so you will remember to update your book. A sample of the spreadsheet can be accessed through our website, *www.threewidows.com*.

The Black Book is an easy way for you to access the information of accounts that need to be closed. Let your personal representatives know where they can find your Black Book, your *I Didn't See That Coming* book (referenced above), and any other critical paperwork.

Shutters and Gutters

What about the household things your husband took care of? Have you thought about who will change your lightbulbs, turn on your well, change your furnace filters (and what size filters you need), check carbon monoxide monitors and smoke alarms, perform lawn and yard maintenance, and change batteries? Can you handle these chores yourself, or do you need someone to help you? Can you invite a neighbor for a "beer and battery check"?

Your Home and Its Mechanics

+ Learn where your main water valve is and how to turn it off.

+ Turn off all outside water faucets and unhook the hoses before going on vacation or before winter. Even if you have frost-proof water faucets, water in a hose can cause the line to freeze and break.

+ Do you need to add security to your home, such as motion sensor spotlights, video doorbells, and the like?

+ Learn where your electrical box or panel is, what it does, and how it works.

+ Does your house use gas? Where is the shutoff valve? Do you need to change tanks or order propane?

+ How often do you have to change furnace filters? Change batteries in alarm systems?

+ Do you have a sump pump or a well pump? Learn how to turn it on and off. One of our survey respondents' husbands died during a derecho. She was without electricity and had no way to contact relatives. A relative showed up unexpectedly to take care of it for her, but once the electricity returned, she didn't know how to turn on her well pump.

+ Keep the manuals for your appliances, big and small, in an easily accessible place. They will prove helpful in a stressful mechanical breakdown. Need hard copies of those manuals? Download and print them from the internet. Put them into the box. (If you decide to move later, the box is a convenient gift for the new homeowners.)

+ Learn the nuts and bolts of your home and the maintenance schedules for all things mechanical, or at least learn what to look for and ask about. Consider hiring professionals to perform maintenance checks on your primary home systems every six months, such as your furnace and air conditioning.

+ Even if your husband writes down instructions, make sure you understand them. It's possible that they are written in his way of understanding, which may not be clear.

Our example: Tall Karen's current husband is an engineer, so when he gives instructions, they can be difficult for the average person to understand. Karen attempted to review the household generator instructions he had written but stopped after the second line because they were not clear. Instead, she rewrote them in an easier way for her to follow. For example, his instruction of "2) Ensure generator has adequate fuel supply" was changed to "2) Hook up the gas line between the house and generator: get the large yellow hose that is hanging below the electric panel downstairs, plug it into the large plug located on the patio wall (metal end slides up, locks generator cord into place), then plug the other end into the generator." These revised instructions were much clearer and easier for Karen to understand, making it simple for her to know what to do.

Yards

Are you interested in yard work? Do you have a lawn mower or snowblower? Do you know how to use them? Do you enjoy weeding and pruning gardens and trees? Are you able to do the edging and weed whacking required with a yard? If not, consider hiring someone else to handle the yard work. Quite a few of our respondents moved to communities or condos where the homeowners association did the yard work.

Our example: After Frank died, Rebecca's neighbor took over snow-blowing duties. She hired a weekly lawn service to mow her large yard.

Cars

If you drive a car without a message system to tell you when maintenance is due, familiarize yourself with the owner's manual. Following the suggested recommendations for car care will keep your vehicle functioning with minimal stress.

A regular oil change is the most important aspect of keeping your car running smoothly and for a long time. An auto maintenance company such as a local mechanic is a good option for regular maintenance, including changing oil, checking various filters, fluids, and tire pressure, and other important maintenance areas. Many of them will leave a sticker on your windshield with the mileage suggestion for the next maintenance; another option is to use the "Trip B" setting of your trip mileage to keep track, resetting after each checkup. Some automotive supply stores may even install the windshield wipers for you if you purchased the wipers from their shop.

It is essential to have your car inspected before embarking on a long journey, paying close attention to fluids and tires. You want to make sure you're prepared.

□   □   □

PART THREE

You, the Widow Among Us

We've discussed being prepared for your legal issues, finances, and home. All the preparation in the world will not take away the difficult experience of being widowed. As we have shared, not all widows have the same experiences. However, here are some aspects of widowhood that you may not understand or that are unsettling. This section is for you, the widow among us, to help you through your challenges.

We understand that early widowhood can be overwhelming. You can download a checklist from our website that will help you address important tasks. *www.threewidows.com*

This section is about caring for YOU. How do you care for yourself?

Brain Fog

Let's talk about "brain fog," which has also been called "widow fog," or "grief fog." The first thing to know about brain fog is that it is NOT a mental health disorder. Brain fog is a physiologic process that occurs during emotional or physical trauma. The brain interprets grief as trauma. The body is flooded with stress hormones. The effects of stress hormones include changes in heart rate, blood pressure, and the brain's ability to process or retain information.

The sad irony is that at the very moments the widow needs her most potent mental energies to handle everything related to the spouse's death, a physiologic survival process hinders her. Because of brain fog and its effects on decision making, widows are often advised not to make crucial decisions (such as selling their homes) for at least a year. While the advice may be sound for some, it is necessary to note that the widow's financial circumstances may require an immediate decision.

In the immediate throes of brain fog, your best plan is to have someone accompany you to important meetings. Let these people serve as your "second set of ears" and take notes. You will have their written documentation and their memory to assist you in making important decisions or carrying out essential actions. If a "second set of ears" isn't possible, designate and label a notebook to carry with you for notetaking. Don't trust your memory—write everything down, even what you might think are small things.

Professionals will recommend that widows read books about grief to ease brain fog. Yet, most widows we surveyed stated they would not have read anything about being a widow, nor could they read books about grieving, for many months. Other suggestions have included mindfulness, journaling, meditation, or engaging in creative endeavors. Many of the widows we surveyed did not have the mental energy to consider engaging in these activities until several months after the spouse's death, if ever. Most didn't have the energy in the early months because they were involved in living through, as Joyce Carol Oates describes, "death duties." As one widow told us, "I *was* the book."

We, too, experienced brain fog.

> *"People thought I was functioning and thinking clearly.*
> *They had no idea."*
> (Karens and Rebecca)

The good news is that brain fog, often caused by stress and elevated stress hormone levels, eventually fades away as these factors decrease. This relief from brain fog can reinvigorate a sense of hope and optimism. You, the widow, will feel more at ease and find reconnecting with your family, friends, and community easier.

Self-Care

It has been projected that a widow will most likely spend five hundred hours completing all the duties required by the death of her spouse. Compared to a forty-hour work week, the widow will work for twelve and a half weeks, slightly over three months. Talking with lawyers, financial advisors, accountants, financial institutions, insurance companies, funeral directors, and probate courts, tracking down paperwork, making multiple decisions, and more may deplete her energy mentally and physically. At the end of this seemingly never-ending process, the widow may feel a "crash." The crucial jobs that were crushing with specific timelines are completed. She may ask, "What do I have to do next?"

It was during this three- to four-month time period after the death that many of the widows we interviewed entered "a dark period." They were exhausted and felt an emotional "letdown." They had even less energy to ask for help. How can a widow care for her health and well-being when she has no mental or physical energy reserves? This was when friends played an essential role in the widows' health.

Physical self-care is a powerful tool that requires nutritious food, hydration, and sleep. The widows we talked with—as well as ourselves—reported erratic sleep in the early months after their spouses' passing. Sleep is essential for optimal health and energy. If the widow struggles to sleep, her stress hormone levels may increase, bringing health problems to light. There are many non-medical ways to initiate sleep, including sleep apps, meditation apps, and white noise machines that can be used to relax and induce sleep. Daytime exercise and reading before bedtime may also assist with this self-care routine, empowering you to take control of your health and well-being.

Sunshine, fresh air, deep breaths, and movement can elevate your mood. Even spending five minutes on your porch in the morning, watching the sun creep across your neighborhood, helps to briefly break the cycle of grief. A few deep breaths as you listen for bird calls provide a focus for short bursts of gratitude and, perhaps, awe. Walking down your block alone, with a friend or a dog, can break the cycle of ruminating thoughts for a few moments. Movement briefly focuses your attention on your body and gets you "out of your head."

Can you find a reason to smile or laugh? In her story, Rebecca recounted how two punsters caused her to laugh daily.

Talking About It

There is no prescription for whether or not you need to talk with anyone about your feelings during caregiving or grief. Some people prefer to manage their thoughts and feelings by themselves. Some have close friends or family with whom they discuss the hardships, challenges, and emotions.

You may want to join a caregivers' group or talk with a professional religious leader or counselor. There is no correct answer. If you try something and it doesn't work, think carefully about whether it is worth your time and energy to continue.

Joining a Facebook or social media group for and with widows may be a good idea. You may be able to share in experiences, lift each other up, and support each other when needed. However, be cognizant of the overall mood of the group. In some instances, the members focus on their loss, depression, and overall hardships. It's important to seek support from others during the process, rather than being surrounded by constant negativity that can bring you down.

Solving Healthcare Dilemmas

It is a well-known fact that healthcare providers often overlook women's health complaints. If the widow is also an older woman, she can become a victim of medical ageism. She may be dismissed with the assumption that her health concerns are due to "getting older," regardless of her actual age or activity levels. Advocating for one's health can consume a lot of physical and emotional energy, which the widow may not have in reserve. This is a crucial time for having that "second set of ears." Bring someone along with you to the medical appointments. Ask them to help you ask the questions you want answered. Have them write down the answers in a notebook so you can refer to the information later. And if you cannot get the answers or the care you need, consider finding another physician.

Feelings

The feelings experienced by the widows we surveyed were quite similar. However, they were felt at different times, in different intensities, and for differing lengths of time. The widows' feelings and emotions powerfully influenced their energy levels, interactions with others, and even their self-care. Yet, their interactions with others and how well they cared for themselves also influenced their emotions and feelings. The emotional swing and frequent dramatic changes are not uncommon in widowhood. They are a natural reaction to the trauma of loss.

A Caretaker's Gradual Loss

Life changes gradually for the spouse of someone with a long-term illness. There is a constant awareness that, eventually, you will be facing widowhood. Widows who shared their stories expressed heightened feelings of sadness and a heavy sense of impending change.

Witnessing their spouse's vibrant presence diminish daily was painful. As they assumed more caretaking responsibilities, they felt a growing sense of aloneness and were saddened by the fading quality of spousal companionship.

Spousal caregivers also reported experiencing a loss of confidence, especially if they lacked formal education or training in healthcare and medication administration. The burden of caregiving amplifies stress levels while sapping energy and vitality, leaving caregivers feeling drained.

After the passing of their spouses, the widows expressed a sense of relief from their burdens. They described the feeling of being able to take a deep breath. However, alongside this sense of release, they also grappled with the daunting prospect of facing life alone.

Anticipatory Grief

There is a significant difference between the grief experienced with the sudden loss of your spouse and learning that your spouse has a prolonged illness. During anticipatory grief, a dark cloud looms on the distant horizon, casting ominous shadows overhead.

Learning that your spouse will be gone at some unknown time in the future throws your life into chaos. That unknowing is so hard.

Every woman will cope with her impending loss differently. It's difficult to manage. Grief can surface in small doses at unwanted and irregular times.

Being Alone

Many widows described being alone in similar ways, emphasizing that being alone doesn't necessarily translate to feeling lonely. They expressed that being alone meant not having someone to share their daily life with or having a familiar companion to accompany them throughout the day. They mentioned the absence of shared experiences, such as not being able to share morning coffee or discuss experiences with someone else. However, they humorously pointed out that being alone also allowed them to indulge in unconventional dinner choices like popcorn and ice cream if they so desired.

Another side of being alone is having to make decisions by oneself. Numerous widows shared feelings of insecurity and doubt when it came to making decisions independently. They often felt anxious and uncertain about their choices, fearing that they might make mistakes. However, they failed to realize that they were actually making well-informed decisions based on the available information.

Reframing Guilt

Reframing is simply seeing or understanding something in a new way, allowing you to see an event from a different point of view. Think of it as looking through a camera lens; the picture is different if you zoom in close or out to a great distance.

Our survey respondents frequently mentioned guilt about their spouses' dying moments. The cause of these feelings was not being able to stay with their spouse during the final death experience. The widows felt they "should" have been able to stay with the spouse. Let us analyze some ideas regarding the origins of this guilt.

Society has romanticized the idea of a spouse crawling into bed with the dying person—to be with them until the end. The movie *Love*

Story and the novel *The Notebook* are examples. Yet, romance doesn't tell the truth about the dying experience. Rarely is death a soft and gentle passage.

When someone is dying, a few individuals can provide support and comfort until the end, even if the passing is not peaceful. But for the most part, people are not equipped to handle the challenges of the dying process and often end up feeling regretful for something they could not have known or experienced before.

It is possible that feeling guilty, or even ashamed, in the aftermath of a spouse's death may stem from a concern over others' thoughts or expectations. However, it is important to remember that it is not the privilege of others to impose their expectations or judgments on the widow. This is a deeply personal and sensitive experience, and the widow should not feel burdened by the opinions of others.

Feeling guilty is not a productive use of your precious energy. Such feelings lead to self-punishment, especially when your brain and body are already affected by the hormonal effects of trauma. For your own well-being, try to see the situation from a different perspective and acknowledge that you did the best you could with the knowledge and love that you had.

Self-Preservation and Protecting Others

Many widows reported expending energy controlling information about themselves and their perceived "weaknesses." They also expended energy trying to protect the reputation of the deceased spouse. The widows didn't want others to change their image of the husband; they didn't want to verbalize that the husband was getting weaker or had flaws. They were held back by their own fears about other people's judgments of them and their spouses. They tried to protect themselves by controlling the emotional milieu and the story around them.

Allowing yourself to experience vulnerability during uncertainty, emotional pain, and exposure is not a sign of weakness. It is the crack in your wall that lets others see your pain. It is the opening that allows others to step forward and support you as you need. And even if you, the widow, did "fall apart" for a time, how does that brief period of "falling apart" matter in a lifetime of days?

As difficult as it might be, allow yourself to be vulnerable and ask for help as needed. Be gracious to yourself as the widow. Allow others to help you as you would help others in need.

Friends and Family

Not all families are supportive of widows. Some widows have faced terrible judgment and behavior from their extended families. They have been accused of not grieving enough, told whom they are allowed to date, and even threatened with disinheritance if they remarry. This kind of interference only adds to the stress the widow is already experiencing. As the women talked more about this, they often found the accusations were voiced by people feeling guilty because they had not been involved in the care of a dying spouse. Others were unaware of what life had been like for the couple or felt an unwarranted sense of control toward the widow.

However, most widows interviewed and surveyed noted they received support from most of their friends. They did mention that "friendships will change over time. Some friends will leave you, some you will leave, some will step up, and some will leave something on your doorstep and call ten days later." Some people can't handle the messiness of life, and you have the choice about whether or not you want to keep the relationship going. Their experiences spoke to truths about friendships.

Some widows choose to expand their social circles because their husbands were antisocial. They talked about the joy of meeting new people and making friends on their own. The widows agreed that there came a time when they realized the enjoyable things they were doing or experiencing would have been completely different if their spouse were still alive. This new positive experience is part of the future they were creating. It's another step forward through grief.

Did You Ever Think There Would Be Another?

This was a lively topic. The most emphatic answer was "Hell no." Older widows (sixty-five years and above) were prone to answer "no" because they didn't want to be a "nurse or a purse." Others had no interest in another relationship.

Some widows did find new love. Yet, once again, they worried about what friends and family would think about them. They feared the judgments of others.

"I didn't tell anybody because it was a year after he died, and I was afraid everybody thought I was a terrible person because it was 'so soon.' However, once people found out, they were thrilled for me, especially women. They loved seeing that I was moving forward. I learned it's not always the expectation others will have about me. It's how I expected others to react, which is often a wrong assumption."

Those widows who had found new loves stated they were very happy. They also recognized that the new love was especially sweet due to the experience and lessons of the earlier marriage. They found partners who honored them as the strong women they had become.

What's Your Name?

It's common for widows who have remarried or found new partners to accidentally call their new partner by the name of their deceased spouse. This can be frustrating or embarrassing for them. However, it's a normal occurrence due to the biology of the brain.

During the course of a relationship, each time a person says their spouse's name, a neuronal pathway is established in the brain. This is similar to a path created in a field by many people walking in the same direction over a long period of time. The more times the spouse's name is said, the stronger the neuronal pathway becomes.

Although the brain can take control when a person wants to say the new partner's name, the nerve messages tend to follow the most established pathway, which is the deceased spouse's name. This is why it's common to accidentally say the wrong name, even if the person is aware of their mistake.

◙   ◙   ◙

Ｙou may know a widow but don't know exactly how you can help her. Here are some ideas and suggestions based on what we learned from our experiences as widows and those of widows we've surveyed and interviewed. On our website, you can download our chart about how to help a widow. *www.threewidows.com*

Our respondents reported, "People don't understand that you aren't thinking like a regular person because of brain fog. Although people tend to withdraw after the first week following a death, widows still require support in the months following the funeral. I wouldn't have eaten if it hadn't been for the food people brought me earlier. Nobody was calling me. Nobody knew I was having difficulty."

Be an Intentional Friend

Is there anything more inconvenient than death? Death can be an overwhelming and demanding trauma, leaving one unaware of how to support the widow or unwilling to deal with the emotional impact of the death.

Intentional friendship is increasing or developing a friendship with purpose and meaning. It is thought out and acted upon. Show up for a friend and delve deeper even though she appears to be "holding her own."

Friends are essential to a widow's well-being. The widow may be exhausted from trying to do too much or so overwhelmed that she can't crawl out of bed, shower, or go to work (let alone grocery shop or cook for herself).

One widow reported that a friend showed up at her house, pulled her out of bed, put her into the shower, fed her breakfast, and then took her to work. Whether the widow worked for five minutes or two hours, the friend was there to take her back home. These friendly interventions continued until the widow could carry out these tasks independently. Others reported friends helping them sort through the deceased spouse's clothes and paperwork. A much-appreciated banana split showed up on the doorstep of another widow.

To be an intentional friend is to acknowledge the struggles of the widow. When you respond to her with empathy and compassion, you support the healing of yourself and the widow.

Help her engage in new experiences that create new memories. They are an essential part of healing after loss. If she loves to travel, encourage her to join you when feasible. If she loves wine or beer, invite her to a tasting or special event. Instead of assuming the role of a rescuer who will "fix" the widow, assist her in transitioning to her new future. Be intentionally supportive with your friendships.

Build a Support Network

The surveyed widows recommended creating a plan with friends and other family members to stay in touch with the widow regularly. It can be overwhelming and tiring for her to receive multiple inquiries or offers of help simultaneously. It may also be inconvenient if many premade dishes arrive at the same time. Make plans behind the scenes by setting up a group text to help. Within this group, plans can be made for who is sending food, stopping by, calling, checking in, etc. Most often, she will appreciate that someone is reaching out without her having to decide what that may look like.

Contact every day from at least one person during the first week or two can be very supportive. Continue the contact for several months or longer. The frequency may reduce, but she will appreciate knowing she is cared for.

Organize delivery of fresh and prepared food for at least six to eight weeks or until the widow asks you to stop. Casseroles, muffins, soups, and salads that can be pulled out of the refrigerator and eaten without any or minimal work are helpful in the first few weeks. Take food that will last. A widow's appetite vacillates from not hungry to ravenous.

Offer to drive her to appointments or go for a drive on a pretty day. Some widows are not ready to drive yet. They don't have the stamina or the focus. An option to get out of the house could be very welcome.

If you or someone you know is handy, offer to do some of the following things:

- Annually check the batteries in the smoke and CO2 alarms.

- Change the chandelier and ceiling fan bulbs.

- Make sure she has a fire extinguisher or fire blanket and knows how to use them.

- Provide one or a few hours of handyman services.

- Provide computer technology support if that's your thing.

Simple acts such as moving the trashcans from the curb back to the garage seem too small to be meaningful. However, when the widow feels that her energy reserves are at an end, your simple act will be a welcome relief.

Condolence Gift Cautions

While there are several thoughtful options available in the condolence industry to express care from afar, nothing replaces the impact of direct human interactions. It's important to provide a widow with the reassurance that caring individuals surround her.

Consider her specific preferences and potential allergies before sending a bouquet of flowers, candy, or a fruit basket. Extend an invitation for a comforting cup of tea, coffee, or a beverage of her choice. A heartfelt phone call is equally appreciated.

Manage Your Expectations About the Widow

Very few widows will feel as you imagine. Every experience of loss is different. Every relationship and every person is unique, so it should not be surprising that her experience of being a widow will be unique as well. Not only is it impossible to imagine how a widow feels, it is unwise to judge how she reacts and acts after her loss. Many widows jump into problem-solving. Perhaps they do so out of necessity. Perhaps it's a coping behavior. Perhaps it's a need to be able to control *something* in their lives.

Avoid judging her behavior. If you think she is trying to escape reality, perhaps you're right. She may need time to subconsciously process her new reality before she can fully grasp its impact. However, perhaps you're wrong. She may choose something that gives her positive energy before tackling the challenges that widowhood requires her to manage.

Respect her grief. Demonstrate your support for her individual "style of grief" and reassure her that living up to society's expectations is not necessary. There is no template for grieving.

Be a Light for a Foggy Brain

Brain fog is real and a physiological response to traumas, including grief. Be understanding and support a widow experiencing brain fog. She has trouble concentrating and frequently forgets important information.

Volunteer to accompany her to important appointments with doctors, lawyers, accountants, etc. as a "second set of ears." Pay attention and take good notes for her so she has the information available at later dates.

Remember with Her

Remember to call on special days. She is aware of the person she has lost and wants to know that others also valued him. You're not going to remind her of her loss. She lives with it every day. Gently find a way to let her know you care.

She will want to hear stories about her spouse. Share your funny stories and experiences. Many widows reported that people tried to make them feel happy. It was as if not speaking about the deceased spouse and having only "cheerful" conversations were required to "heal" the widow's grief.

One of our respondents had been a widow for twenty years. After talking with her, she approached us with tears and said, "In twenty years, no one ever asked me to talk about my experience of being a widow. Thank you for asking me." At that moment, we deepened our understanding of how easily our society believes grief is a "one-and-done" event.

Remembrances of how her spouse touched *your* life can be comforting. She may enjoy your sharing stories of the favorite things you loved about her spouse. If you had known her spouse for several years, you may have shared some ridiculous moments, embarrassing circumstances, or crazy adventures. Perhaps you were lucky enough to have experienced all of those. Some widows appreciate seeing other people honestly grieving for their husbands, but not to the extent that the widow ends up comforting others.

Was her spouse an inspiration in some way? Was he a mentor, problem-solver, teacher, or provider of insight? Those stories will be welcomed as confirmations of his impact and place in the world.

> *"While visiting my stepdaughter and son-in-law,*
> *we shared stories about Frank that made us all laugh.*
> *His musical tastes ran to opera and 'head-banging metal*
> *hard rock.' We laughed uproariously about the opera-loving,*
> *deeply respected scientist who was a head-banger."*
> —Rebecca

Reach Out

One of the worst things you can say, even if you're sincere, is, "Call me if you need anything." A widow will most likely not call. Making that phone call would be too overwhelming for her—not only to make the call but to think about what she might need. Instead, she would appreciate it if you called her.

Ask her, "Do you want to be hugged, heard, or helped?" If she says helped, it will be easier for her to accept an offer, rather than think about what she needs. You could say, "I'm going to the grocery store. Can I bring you coffee, milk, eggs, bread, ice cream, or Tylenol?" Or you could call and say, "I just made a pan of lasagna. Can I bring over two meals' worth? Would you like some garlic bread, too? How about a bottle of wine?"

Shopping for groceries and cooking for herself requires energy a widow may not have to spare. The widow is mentally and physically exhausted. Ask about food preferences, however. Some people may have dietary restrictions or just don't like certain foods.

Ensure that she has the opportunity to spend the holidays or special occasions with someone and not be alone unless that is her preference. Tell her she's free to change her mind, and ask again when the occasion is closer. Reassure her that you would relish her company. Don't try to make her feel better or happy—you can't.

Offer opportunities to join you at some of the organizations or events she used to attend. Invite her to get involved in new ventures, classes, or meetings where others will be welcoming. What you think will interest her, however, may not be enthralling or even tolerable at the moment. Congratulate her for trying. Even if a widow declines four out of five times, or if she wants to leave early, don't stop including her or offering to make plans.

One widow said the best thing she ever heard was, "I don't know what to say, but I'm here." The speaker then held her hand and simply sat with her in silence. "It was great to know that someone was there for me, even if neither of us had anything to say."

If you have something in mind, just do it. Don't hesitate because you don't feel close enough to the widow to run an errand. Call her. Don't wait for a widow to call you.

Stay in Touch

It's hard to lose friends and relationships at the same time you lose a spouse. Widows experience a change in identity when they are no longer part of a couple. Friends may fade away because they were closer to her spouse or because they are uncomfortable with seeing only the widow. Find ways to let her know she is valued as an individual and special to you.

A month or two after the funeral, widows may continue to need connections because most people back away after the immediacy of the death. Provide attentive awareness until she tells you she doesn't need whatever special care it is you've been providing. Nurture your friendship in new and different ways.

Ask gentle questions without pushing. Let her carry the conversation. Allow her to talk about her loss, her husband, her challenges, or her feelings.

She's still one of the friends or guests you've always loved to have involved in dinner conversations. Invite her for dinner. She may prefer being a "third wheel" to being ignored and feeling forgotten.

Ask her to join you for a glass of afternoon wine or a morning cup of coffee on the deck. Be silent and listen to the world around you. Let her ramble through her thoughts, and be a silent listener. Take a walk outdoors, if she's up for it.

When you don't know what to say, simply buy and send a greeting card. The words are provided. Finish with an "I'm thinking of you" and your signature.

If you know her style of humor, share things that will make her laugh. Laughter is healing, even for a brief moment. It's not wrong to laugh during grief.

Your friend may temporarily lose interest in things she used to enjoy. Even the book-a-week friend may not be interested in reading. Recognize this is a normal process, and support her choices.

Let Her Decide Her New Future

Let her decide when it's time to focus on creating her new future. Understand that building her subsequent life will be a process only she can manage.

It is important to understand that certain events can trigger grief, even for women who have been widows for many years. These events may include the deaths of close friends or family members, anniversaries, or weddings when the widow realizes that her daughters won't have their dad to walk them down the aisle. It is important to note that the widow is not feeling sorry for herself but is actually experiencing genuine grief.

Refrain from trying to find a new partner for a widow unless she explicitly asks for your help. Numerous widows have shared their discomfort when friends attempted to set them up with new partners, despite their lack of interest. You might not fully comprehend her individual needs. Remember that it's not your duty to fix the widow's grief. Instead, if you decide to take on the role, your responsibility is to provide support, recognize her grieving journey, and offer your presence during this difficult time.

Think Twice About . . .

- Avoid saying, "Everything will be all right." You have no way of knowing what her future holds.

- Avoid making statements like "I know how sad you are" or "I know you must miss him." Don't assume you know how the loss of her spouse affected her and her life.

- Don't offer your perspective that she should "remember the good times" with her spouse. Two widows recounted, "It pissed me off when they tried to tell me we had good times. They didn't live my life."

- Don't tell a widow to "move on." Doing so suggests that it's time to overcome her grief and trauma. Some people fail to understand that a widow's connection with her deceased spouse is never truly over. Everything in her current life was seeded in the years with her spouse and continues. Her life trajectory has been forever altered. Despite the loss of her spouse, his presence continues through their children or the memories she holds dear.

+ Don't say her spouse is in a better place or is now with God. One widow said, "Call me selfish, but I didn't give a damn about his 'other callings' on the day of his funeral—I wanted him back with me!"

+ Even though you want to empathize with the widow and express an understanding of grief, she doesn't want to hear about how you lost your grandmother, father, or dog. Being widowed is very different.

+ Be mindful of long hugs and conversations. One widow commented that people often hugged her too long before letting go and "held me hostage in conversation." Touch can be very healing for humans, but it can also be unwelcome. Be sensitive to her unspoken responses.

+ Don't assume the widow is surrounded by attentive loved ones. You can ask if she would enjoy company or prefer to be alone.

+ Don't ask how her husband died. If she wants to tell you, she will. It's a private story.

+ If you comment about how brave and strong she is, be aware that she is just doing what she must do to manage her circumstances. She may be brave and strong, but she is also in the process of grieving.

+ Don't try to help by suggesting to the widow what she needs to be doing, thinking, or feeling. There is no timetable for when she needs to dispose of his stuff, clean out his closet, move on with her life, get over her grief, or any other behavior you feel would be best. What's best is for you to support her as she moves forward at her own pace.

◘   ◘   ◘

Final Words

When we first considered writing this book in Sedona, we had no idea what we were getting into. The process turned out to be a profound and emotional experience. We opened up to each other, shared our grief, and found catharsis in our conversations. We reassured each other and expressed our worries, concerns, and fears. Instead of trying to overcome our grief, we built lives alongside it. In short, we experienced the value of intentional friendship, even in the years after becoming widows.

After listening to the experiences of other widows, we gained an even deeper understanding of the challenges and emotional impact of grief. We realized that many mothers and grandmothers had never shared their widowhood experiences, and that very few women have the information to face the difficulties of being widowed.

Today, widowhood is still a sensitive and frequently neglected subject. This book aims to bring this important topic into the spotlight by highlighting and addressing its unique and often disregarded aspects.

As we developed this book, it became obvious to us that the kintsugi pot was the perfect metaphor for what we hoped to share with readers about the experience of being a widow. Kintsugi is the practice of mending broken areas with a specialized sap and the dust of precious metals.

Kintsugi is a philosophy that embraces breakage and repair as part of an object's history, rather than something to hide. It celebrates the beauty in broken things, highlighting cracks and repairs as events in an object's life, rather than the end of its usefulness. It's about accepting change and seeing the repaired piece as even more beautiful, revitalized with a new look and given a second life. It's about embracing the beauty of human fragility.

A widow is like a living version of the kintsugi pot. She has been broken open by the death of her spouse. As she moves through her grief process, she has the choice to start repairing the cracks she has experienced with confidence, support, and opportunity. Because she has experienced a most fragile state, she often chooses to revitalize herself for a new and different future.

Brava, Ladies, Brava!

❏ ❏ ❏

Resources

+ Consumer Finance Protection Board, Taking Control of Your Finances: Help for surviving spouses. This step-by-step guide is designed to help you do the most important and pressing things first. https://files.consumerfinance.gov/f /documents/cfpb_surviving-spouse_booklet.pdf

+ Consumer Finance Protection Board, "When a loved one dies and debt collectors come calling." Learn about your debt collection rights as a survivor. https://www.consumerfinance .gov/consumer-tools/educator-tools/resources-for-older-adults /financial-security-as-you-age/when-a-loved-one-dies-and -debt-collectors-come-calling/

+ Justice, Karen S. Justice Scholarship for Study Abroad. For information about applications, contact https://www. frederickcountygives.org/ To donate, https://www.frederick countygives.org/give/#give-now

+ Justice, Karen S. "Transformative Change," blog post. https:// karenjustice.us/2023/01/06/transformative-change/

+ Smith, Karen, R. *I Didn't See* That *Coming! Your Guide to Organizing Your Documents for an Unexpected Life Event.* https://www.amazon.com/I-Didnt-See-That-Coming /dp/0999466003

+ *Spoonful of Comfort.* www.spoonfulofcomfort.com Gourmet Soups Delivered Anywhere.

+ "Volunteering and Its Surprising Benefits," https://www.helpguide .org/articles/healthy-living/volunteering-and-its-surprising -benefits.htm

References

Kiplinger Personal Finance. www.kiplinger.com/personal-finance/602892 /widows-move-forward-on-their-own-but-not-alone.

Thrivent. Survey completed in May 2024.

Credits for Photos
and Illustrations

Page 1: Three Windows into Widowhood, Illustration by Rebecca LaChance.

Page 2: Sam and Karen Smith, personal collection.

Page 38: Karen and John Justice, personal collection.

Page 86: Frank Lebeda and Rebecca LaChance, personal collection.

Page 128: The Grief Balloon and Button, illustration by Rebecca LaChance, adapted from Lauren Herschel.

Page 129: Topics That Worried Our Survey Respondents Most, Illustration by Rebecca LaChance.

Page 143: You, the Widow Among Us, Canva

Page 157: How to Help a Widow, illustration by Rebecca LaChance.

Page 172: The Kintsugi Pot, illustration by Rebecca LaChance.

Page 187: Karen Smith-Racicot, author photo, photo by Rebecca LaChance.

Page 188: Karen Justice, author photo, photo by Rebecca LaChance.

Page 189: Rebecca LaChance, author photo, personal collection.

Acknowledgments

In many ways, a book is like a child—it takes a village to raise one. Many "villagers" supported us through this process.

As co-authors, we acknowledge that merging the thoughts, personalities, and writing styles of three individuals into a coherent and meaningful book is not an easy task. Despite the challenges, we believed in the value of our stories and persevered through our differences to create a book that we hope will resonate with others. *(Pardon us a moment while we share a well-deserved high-five.)*

We also thank our beta readers and reviewers whose input helped improve our book and provided thoughtful comments.

A big shoutout to the Steve Harrison National Publicity Summit for our education about working with the media, and the opportunity to do so.

We truly appreciate the professionalism and expertise exhibited by the 1106 Design team. Their impressive, impactful cover design and interior layout, as well as their excellent communication throughout the process, have made our experience exceptionally smooth and satisfying.

Rebecca

I would like to express my gratitude to my sister, Anita Aycock, and brother-in-law, Brian Aycock, for their unwavering support throughout the creation of this book. My sister was my sounding board as I delved into my memories of our mother, and her insights were invaluable. Additionally, during a scary medical procedure, they took care of both me and my dog, providing comfort and care while I recovered. Their love and support mean the world to me, and I am incredibly grateful to have them in my life.

Karen Smith Racicot

I don't know where I'd be without my girls—Shannon, Jessica, and Danielle—who have always loved, supported, and challenged me to be my best. They are my inspiration. My mom is my biggest cheerleader, supporting my many endeavors and inspiring me to live life to the fullest by her wonderful example. I am so grateful that Bob came into my life. He encourages me in every way, and I love that we can explore life side by side.

Karen Justice

While it may seem unusual to acknowledge your co-authors, I wish to do so because our teamwork made my work better. They not only pushed me beyond my comfort level at times, they opened doors to personal insights and revelations. I want to acknowledge my friend and mini cheering squad, Marie Beck, for her belief and encouragement. I especially want to acknowledge my life partner, Jeff Rock, who shared his business insight and personal support. His confidence in our success pulled me through the challenges of this project.

Message from the Authors

Engage with Us

Are you interested in discussing our experiences or the book? We are available for book signings, speaking engagements, and discussions. Please contact us at *info@threewidows.com* or visit our website at *www.threewidows.com*.

Speaking opportunities and topics:

- ✦ Presentations to your group
- ✦ Discussions with your book club in person or via Zoom

Using our stories as examples, we converse with your audience about:

- ✦ The different grief experiences
- ✦ The importance of self-care for the widow
- ✦ Practical ways for loved ones to support grief recovery

- ✦ How life can be beautiful again as it leads you to a new future

- ✦ Being prepared for the undesired circumstance of being widowed

- ✦ A widow's holidays

- ✦ Ways to travel when you live alone

- ✦ Cooking for one

We answer your questions about our stories, preparations, decisions, other topics, and more. We've lived it. Just ask us. *www.threewidows.com/contact*

Support Our Valuable Message

Please take a moment and review our book on Amazon or Goodreads to help other women discover what you've learned. Help us shine the light on the hidden aspects of widowhood. Recommend our book to your family, friends, and community.

If you only have time to say, "This is a well-written, informative book," that's fine. You may also want to comment about:

+ Who you think would benefit from reading this book.

+ How you connected with any of the three stories.

+ The piece or part of the book you especially liked.

Just for fun, drop us a line through our website and tell us which actress you think should play each author's part if the book becomes a movie! *www.threewidows.com/contact*

Book Club Questions

1. Did you notice any similarities in how the three widows expressed their grief?

2. What factors do you believe had the greatest impact on Tall Karen's path to confidence?

3. Tall Karen shared her thoughts on never having those important "what-if" conversations with Sam about their lives and business. In what specific ways can her insights benefit individuals who need to engage in the "what-if" discussions?

4. Short Karen and Rebecca discussed not giving people enough credit or trying to protect them from information about their late husbands' deaths. Is this response specific to only these two women, or does it apply more broadly? Also, how and why do you try to protect others?

5. Grief, often perceived as a singular experience, is a universal emotion. What insights did you gain about this universal emotion from the three widows?

6. Short Karen's early years were marked by frequent relocations due to her family's circumstances. After marrying a military man, she continued to experience the upheaval of moving to new homes. Do you believe that her lifetime of adjusting to new environments might have impacted her approach to coping with loss?

7. Rebecca opened up about the ways in which her neurodivergence affected her experience of grieving. She noted that others judged her grief without considering or understanding the impact of her unique neurological traits. How do you interpret her story in relation to your interactions with others?

8. With an estimated one million women in the U.S. becoming widows each year, it's notable that there hasn't been a substantial proactive conversation and preparation for widowhood. For mothers, how do you plan to educate your daughters about preparing for widowhood?

9. Explore the changes brought about by the Condolence Gift Industry in providing support to widows during their time of loss. How has it shaped the way people show compassion and understanding?

10. The two Karens both found new love after the passing of their spouses. Do you think they both felt the same apprehension about being scrutinized by others? What do you think motivates some individuals to believe they have the right to interfere in a widow's quest for happiness?

About the Authors

Karen R. Smith-Racicot (Tall Karen) is a certified life coach and co-owned an accounting firm for over twenty years with her late husband. After her husband's untimely death, she authored the workbook *I Didn't See That Coming!* as a guide for organizing important legal, financial, and insurance documents. She has spoken on that topic at various venues in the D.C. metro area.

Karen is remarried and has five adult children/stepchildren and seven grandkids. She loves to quilt, and she and her husband, Bob, enjoy traveling and camping, especially throughout the beautiful U.S. national parks.

Through twenty-nine lifetime moves, Karen S. Justice, MBA (Short Karen), developed skills for facing change. Becoming a widow, however, was one of the most substantial changes she faced. She and John had been married for over forty-seven years. For thirty-one of those, she followed him around the world as a military spouse. Every move required modifying life, jobs, and expectations.

After her husband's death, Karen again modified her expectations and focused on building a new future. The effort combined fear, freedom, excitement, disruption, joy, and sadness. She learned even more about challenges and adaptation to change. Today, Karen continues to use her knowledge and experience through mentoring, teaching, and writing.

Rebecca K. LaChance, PhD, lost her husband of twenty-five years from a heart attack in the early days of COVID-19. Her experience of becoming a widow and grieving was deeply influenced by pandemic restrictions, her  neurodiverse brain, childhood traumas, and her introversion.

She practiced as a registered nurse for over thirty years. Rebecca's specialty was Critical Care. Her academic career focused on the impacts of a significant other's death, including her dissertation about how advance directives were implemented in a military medical hospital.

www.ingramcontent.com/pod-product-compliance
Lightning Source LLC
Chambersburg PA
CBHW060809120626
46557CB00001B/140